TRAVE

The Reverend Margaret Cundiff was born in Somerset but has lived in the north of England since early childhood. Since 1973 she has served on the staff of St James' Church, Selby, in North Yorkshire, and was ordained deacon in 1987. She is also Broadcasting Officer for the diocese of York and broadcasts frequently both locally and nationally. She has contributed regularly to BBC Radio 2's *Pause for Thought*, and to the British Forces Broadcasting Service's religious programmes.

Also by Margaret Cundiff

Called to be Me *and* Following On (*New Bumper Edition*)

I'd Like You to Meet. . .

Living by the Book – *A personal journey through the Sermon on the Mount*

Good Morning – It's Margaret

My Kind of Day

TRAVELLING LIGHT
Through St Mark's Gospel

Margaret Cundiff

*'They travel lightly whom
God's grace carries'*
Thomas à Kempis

Tri∆ngle

First published 1992
Triangle
SPCK
Holy Trinity Church
Marylebone Road
London NW1 4DU

British Library Cataloguing in Publication Data

A catalogue record for this book is available from the British Library

ISBN 0–281–04570–4

Typeset by Inforum Typesetting, Portsmouth
Printed in Great Britain by BPCC Hazel Books,
Aylesbury, Bucks.
Member of BPCC Ltd.

Contents

For my mum and dad,
with my love and thanks
for all they have been, are,
and will be to me –
always.

Acknowledgements

My thanks to Peter, Julian and Alison who have so cheerfully put up with me writing yet another book;

to my Vicar, David, for his patience and prayers, and to all my friends at St James' Church, Selby and in the Diocese of York;

to Fran and Ian, who lovingly and efficiently produced the manuscript on their computer, and to Geoff Green for the delightful cover photograph.

My thanks, too, to all at SPCK for their help and encouragement, and particularly to my former Editor, Myrtle Powley, who has guided me through a decade of writing for Triangle with her wisdom and friendship.

And as this year I celebrate my sixty glorious years' – Thanks be to God!

All Bible quotations are from the *Good News Bible* published by the Bible Societies and Harper Collins, © American Bible Society, New York, 1966, 1971 and 4th edition 1976, with permission. The Collect for St Mark the Evangelist's Day is from *The Alternative Service Book 1980* © The Central Board of Finance of the Church of England.
Other books quoted:
William Barclay, *The Gospel of Mark* (St Andrew Press 1975)
Stuart Blanch, *Encounters with Jesus* (Hodder & Stoughton 1988)
William Clemmons, *Discovering the Depths* (Triangle 1989)
Frank Colquhoun, *Strong Son of God* (Lakeland 1973)
Eddie Gibbs, *Born into Battle*
Morris Maddocks, *The Christian Healing Ministry* (SPCK 1981, 1990)
John Young, *Jesus the Verdict* (Lion 1990)

Introduction

Mark's Gospel is the earliest of the Gospel accounts. It is a fast-moving, straightforward series of 'action shots' giving us a picture of the ministry of Jesus, an introduction to Jesus himself, allowing us to stand alongside him as he meets people, life situations and death itself. Of the sixteen chapters which range over the three years of Jesus' public ministry, the last six are devoted to the events of the last week in his life here on earth. As we read Mark's Gospel we can feel the authentic note. Here is someone who knows what he is talking about, and tells it as it is, without frills. Mark is so anxious to share the story with us that he rushes on, the words tumbling out, flooding over us. But who was this Mark? What right had he to write this Gospel?

We can find out a great deal about Mark as we read the New Testament. He lived in Jerusalem, the son of a well-to-do lady called Mary (Acts 12.12). Their home was a centre for the first Christians, and so Mark was surrounded by those who knew Jesus, who were close to him. He was the nephew (or perhaps cousin) of Barnabas (Colossians 4.10), and so when Paul and Barnabas set out on their first missionary journey, they took Mark along with them (Acts 12.25; 13.5). The trouble was, Mark got homesick and turned back, which caused great disagreement between Paul and Barnabas (Acts 13.13; 15.36–40). Barnabas wanted to give Mark another chance. Paul thought not – he was not going to take someone who wanted to go home to mother when the pace got hot! Nevertheless, later on, when Paul was in prison, he recognised the worth of Mark and asked for him to be brought to help him (2 Timothy 4.11).

The greatest source of the information Mark gathered was from Peter. Mark, it is said, was Peter's interpreter, who sat and wrote down what Peter told him of those three years when he had been part of the inner circle of the disciples, the one in whom Jesus confided and shared with so intimately. Peter was transparently honest with Mark and told him of what had happened, even those painful times when Peter had misunderstood Jesus, had blundered in and even denied him. It must have been a great encouragement to Mark to know that even the great Peter had failed and yet was given another chance, which he had taken with both hands. It is a great encouragement to us too as we look at our own lives, our own times of failure, as well as the times we have gone forward in faith and with clear vision and purpose.

Did Mark ever meet Jesus himself? Where was he as a youngster when Jesus walked the streets of his home city? There is a verse in the Gospel which may give us a clue. When Jesus was arrested in the garden of Gethsemane, amid all the confusion, the shouting and clamour, the disciples running like mad from that place, we are told: 'A certain young man dressed only in a linen cloth, was following Jesus. They tried to arrest him, but he ran away naked, leaving the cloth behind' (Mark 14.51–52). 'A certain young man' – was Mark speaking of himself? It seems more than likely. He ran away then, he ran home when he found being in the hot seat with Barnabas and Paul too much to cope with; but he grew up, grew up in years, faith and experience, and in his writing he gives us this precious gift of a faithful record of what happened two thousand years ago when Jesus walked on this earth, meeting ordinary people, just like you and me, bringing them good news of God's love and purpose, a message of forgiveness, of victory, of healing and peace.

Here in this Gospel account we will discover for ourselves that good news, and how people reacted to it. For the purpose of my book I have used the Good News Bible, but of course you can follow it in any of the many translations and versions available. I often find it helpful to compare one version with another, but that is up to you. The main thing is that you do read the actual text.

What sort of response did Jesus get? What happened to him? Mark is eager to tell us, to share the story with us. So then, come with him, and share with me too, as together we journey through his account, the Gospel according to Mark.

Lord Jesus,
As we begin our journey,
go with us,
help us to see and hear
and understand,
and make our response
to you.

3

This is it!
(1.1)

It is not often that a sermon preached on a Sunday makes headlines in the press on Monday, or is deemed worthy of a mention on radio or television the following day – not even when the preacher is an archbishop, or the place a crowded cathedral. A notable exception was a sermon preached in York Minster on 24th February 1980 by the then Archbishop of York, Dr Stuart Blanch. In it he appealed for more cheeful items to be included in television news bulletins, saying he had given up watching the news at night. 'Earlier in the day I might be able to take it,' he said, 'but at night it is altogether too much for me, the endless repetition of violence, intended or achieved, strident speeches, declaration of war, flying pickets equipped with everything except wings, and an unwholesome atmosphere of unrest and confusion.'

His sermon certainly caught the headlines, and caused much comment, particularly from the media men, like, 'I am dismayed the Archbishop does not recognise that our task is to convey, not to censor information to a perceptive and mature society . . . We cannot close our eyes to what is going on all over the world . . .' Another news editor said, 'We agree that so much of the news these days is gloomy . . .', and yet another editorial: 'The difficulty for anyone attempting to strike a balance between news items, as any chief subeditor will tell you, is that on a busy news day there happens to be rather a lot of it. Hence the practical view is taken that if an item interests a majority of readers, it must be given prominence. There is little or no time to compose one's views on what the world really should be like and make up a page or a bulletin accordingly.' Many other comments were in similar vein; the Archbishop had touched on a raw spot I think!

To be fair, there did seem to be an effort made to include some good news for a while, with lots of fun remarks, and an excellent 'Giles' cartoon, which gave the Archbishop something to laugh about. That was over ten years ago. Has anything changed? Reading the papers, listening to radio and watching television, I think not. But then the world is a tough place, you could say a hopeless place, full of bad news. Yet at the same time there is an enormous amount of good happening, although not always considered newsworthy, because it is 'ordinary' – and that fact alone should be seen as good news!

Mark, writing his Gospel, has no problem about what is and what is not good or bad news, he starts straight in. 'This is the Good News about Jesus Christ, the Son of God . . .' Good news, not to be tagged on as an end item to make us feel comfortable as we switch off the television set and make our way to bed. Not there to create balance, so as not to get a one-sided view of life, not to act as an 'and they lived happily ever after' ending to cheer up those who found life all too much; but genuine good news, God's good news, in person! A person who actually lived, a background that could be tested, examined, and the facts stand up to scrutiny. His name was Jesus, and he stands firm and strong today, for he is as he always was the Son of God. He came and preached the good news from God, offered the good news to all who would be prepared to hear it. No one would be excluded from receiving it, by colour, culture, age, ability or background, by what they had been or what they were. No one was barred from the good news. It was good news, pure and simple, and no small print!

'Here is the good news,' says Mark, as he points us to Jesus Christ, the Son of God. Are you willing then to read, to see, to hear? Are you brave enough to follow it through? Be warned – all will be revealed, and you may find it hard sometimes to bear the truth. But if you are willing and open enough to try, then you will come face to face with the good news, will be able to make your own decision on it, and on whether you want to share that good news with others.

As I write this I have a daily newspaper beside me, open at one of the sports pages, and telling of the world of top-class athletics. It mentions a young man called Jon Edwards, Britain's top triple jumper, and the meeting that, although most young athletes would give their back teeth to be allowed to have the honour of being at it, he has declined to take part in. Why? As a committed Christian he refuses not only to compete, but to train, on Sundays. The reporter obviously found it hard to understand Jon's reasons, as he cheerfully but very definitely put his case: 'I have priorities in my life, the first is God, second my family and third my sport.'

Jon is only one such young man who puts God first in his life, and follows it through, whatever it costs. I meet people every day whose lives may not make the front or back pages of any national, or even local paper, but who live out their faith with joy, who have discovered the good news in Jesus Christ, the Son of God, who own him as their Saviour, their Master, their God, and their good news. Like Mark they point to him, so that we may read the good news clothed in the flesh of today's experiences. Let us then read on!

Father,
Thank you for the good news you have given to us in your Son, Jesus Christ. For those who have faithfully recorded his life and work so we may read and know.
Thank you for those who today show in their lives the power and the reality of the good news and so encourage us in our understanding and experience.
May the pages of our lives bear the imprint of your love and prove to be good news to those around us.
We ask it for his sake, and in his name.

Clear the Way
(1.2–11)

The evening was so far proving something of a disappointment. It was not as glamorous in the TV studio as the audience had imagined – all rather boring, in fact. There were no famous faces, just people moving cameras and cables about, or wandering around with pieces of paper. When they had applied for tickets all those weeks ago it had been very exciting, the thought of going to see a show 'live', and maybe being picked out by the cameras so friends and relatives at home would see them. Now some folk were muttering, 'It would have been easier to have watched it at home – at least I could have worn my slippers, and nipped out to make a cup of tea.'

Then the lights went on and a man in evening dress took centre stage. Within moments he had captured their attention and their hearts. His quick wit, charm and versatility, pace and pathos, held the audience spellbound. In no time at all he had them all singing along with him, clapping and cheering, and having a great time – that was all before the star of the show appeared and the real business of the evening got under way. By then, the audience had forgotten everything but the sheer joy of being there. Everybody was well and truly in the mood. 'What was that chap's name who came on first, before the show? I can't remember his name, don't think I'd ever seen him before.' He was just the 'warm-up guy', there to pave the way, to make sure the people were ready.

The people who lived in Palestine had got rather tired of waiting for their promised Messiah. It was all well and good what the prophets had said all those years ago, but time had gone by, and no Messiah had appeared. Now they were living under the control of a foreign power. It was every man for himself, 'look after number one', do what you like, who cares – as long as you don't get caught. God himself seemed distant, certainly to the ordinary people, beyond the understanding of mere men and women. Maybe the priests understood, but so many of them were concerned only with matters of politics and of theological argument; there was no direction, no challenge to be different.

Suddenly from out of nowhere a man appeared, a strange-looking man, for all the world like one of the old-time prophets come back to life. He was frightening, powerful. You couldn't help but listen to what he had to say. It was a very simple message: 'Turn away from your sins and be baptised, and God will forgive you.' What he said touched the hearts of people. They recognised that he was from God, that his message was true, and they flocked to him, crying for forgiveness to God, and being baptised in the river Jordan by the man John – whom they called the Baptist.

John had a clear-cut message. Some thought he might really be the Messiah, but he told them firmly he was only a voice, and that someone was coming after him, who was the promised Messiah. Everybody knew that John the Baptist was a good man, unafraid to speak the message God had given him, and it was clear by his life that he lived out the message too. A great man indeed, a leader of men – and yet all the time he was telling them of the greater one to come, so great, so good that he, John, would not even be fit to untie his sandals. This coming one would also baptise people, but not with water, but with the Holy Spirit.

Not long afterwards Jesus did come, and like all the others was baptised by John; but he was different, he was the promised one. John knew that, and announced it to the people. I wonder if they believed him. Could this really be the Promised One, this ordinary-looking man, the carpenter from Nazareth? For Jesus it was the beginning of his public ministry – the beginning of three short years, from the water of the Jordan to the water of death. At that moment of baptism Jesus knew in a powerful, personal way the annointing from his Father with the Holy Spirit, in the river of Jordan.

As for John, the 'warm-up guy', his main work was finished. He had done the job God had given him to do, and he had done it well. His reward? – prison, for upsetting Herod. Never again would he know the freedom of the countryside, the clean fresh air, the hills and the sea, never again baptise in the Jordan. Prison and death, that was the lot of John. Where was God in all that? What use was the Messiah to John when he was chained up like some animal? No divine rescue mission was launched for him.

God still calls 'warm-up guys' – and women too. By their quality of life, their obedience and humility, they clear the way for the good news. They are those who without fear or favour deliver God's word, not to attract the crowds, to make a name for themselves, but to point to Jesus. I remember some years ago meeting a man who was so direct in what he said that he got himself into quite a lot of trouble, and made himself rather unpopular. I suggested it might be a bit easier if he toned it down a little; after all, people don't like being told what sinners they are, even if it happens to be true. 'I'm a spiritual gadfly,' he said. 'I nip people with the truth to make them think.' That was his ministry, and he carried it out, because God had called him to do so. He too was a voice, just a voice.

'Warm-up guy' – 'spiritual gadfly' – clearing the way so Jesus can be heard. This is a vital ministry, from the old-time prophets, through to John – and my friend. And thank God for them. We need to hear them, all of them.

Father,
Thank you for your messenger, John the Baptist,
for his courage, holiness and humility. Thank
you for all those who in today's world, are will-
ing to serve as voices, trail blazers, so that Jesus
may be seen and heard and received as Saviour
and Lord.

A Strategy for Life
(1.12–20)

It had been one of those rather frustrating meetings when we had seemed to go round and round in circles, and ever decreasing ones at that. Driving home I turned on the car radio hoping to find some soothing music, but instead I heard a very authoritative voice saying, 'Of course, what you need from the word Go is strategy. Work that out first of all. Then, having established what your objectives are, choose your team with great care. Then you can begin to think about tactics.' I was hooked! I learned a great deal on the drive home, but it was not until the end of the programme that I discovered who the speaker was, a very famous and highly successful captain of industry. He had been talking about his experience in building up a company from nothing to a multinational corporation.

Jesus also built up a company from nothing to a multinational corporation. It has branches everywhere, and although a few areas may seem to be experiencing recession, others are expanding in leaps and bounds. Overall, the Church is claimed to be the fastest-growing mass movement in the world. Jesus knew that strategy was of primary importance. That is why right at the beginning of his ministry, after his baptism and the affirmation of his Father, he went away into the wilderness for a period of forty days. It was a time when he was tempted in a number of ways to take short cuts to his objective, to use his power to satisfy his own needs, to perform sensational 'crowd-pullers' and to compromise his message and mission. It was a testing time, a hard training ground, the tension between God's way and the world's way.

God versus the devil, wild animals versus angels – a very dramatic start to his ministry. But Jesus emerged the victor, for he met temptation with the authoritative 'It is written,' pointing to God's commands, laid down in Scripture. His strategy was formed on the solid ground of the authority of God. He could immediately point to the precise Scripture that dealt with the very question.

Perhaps this is something Christians should pay more attention to when they come up against the temptations of 'the world, the flesh and the devil'! So often I meet Christians who are proud to be called 'people of the Book', but sadly it is a closed book apart from a few favourite passages, random 'proof texts' and half-understood doctrinal teaching. A bishop once remarked grimly that he could tell which year a clergyman had left college by the books on his shelf. Many Christians leave Bible study alone after baptism or confirmation classes, feeling somehow that they know it all and that knowledge will grow without any conscious effort on their part. With so little attention to discipline, training and study, no wonder they cut no ice with questioners, or when challenged to go and share their faith with others, protest lamely, 'But I wouldn't know what to say.' If Jesus needed to discipline himself, to spend time on retreat, to be regular in public as well as private worship and be totally familiar with Scripture, shouldn't that point to the obvious, that those who claim to be his followers should follow his way and learn from his example?

After his experience in the wilderness Jesus knew the course his ministry had to take. He was sure of his strategy, now it had to be worked out.

And so he gathered around him his team, those he would train 'on the job', who would carry on his work when he was no longer with them. These were key positions, so it was vital he got the best, the brightest, the most loyal and durable. 'Head-hunting' is a well-known concept in industry, commerce and academic circles. People of high academic qualifications and proven track record are pursued and wooed, made offers too good to be refused, companies often trying to outbid each other in their determination to attract those potential members for their top team.

Jesus did not go to the top religious and academic centres to try to persuade their brightest and best to join him. He did not paint a picture of glittering prizes ahead. He simply went out with the message of the kingdom of God, the good news of forgiveness, of new life, and invited some local fishermen to join him. Two sets of brothers, Simon and Andrew, James and John, were to become his closest friends and companions. Ordinary working men – but they knew how to catch fish, and Jesus promised them they would catch men too.

I am well acquainted with the ways of fishermen. My son has been a devoted and enthusiastic fisherman since he was a twelve-year-old. Out in all weathers, often going through long patches of catching nothing at all, spending time, effort and his hard-earned money on his hobby, in good times and bad refusing to be beaten, to give up, he takes no heed of those who consider him a fanatic, stupid or even a little crazy. But he knows the joy and excitement of catching fish, the pride in landing a big one, carefully and very lovingly weighing and photographing his catches, the great sense of achievement and personal satisfaction. 'Not so much a hobby, more a way of life,' he tells me!

Through my son I have come to know a lot of fishermen. They all have those same qualities of stickability, determination, and enthusiasm. They study every aspect of fishing – water and weather conditions, the habits of fish – you could say they can almost read what is going on inside the minds of fish! They know what attracts them, each fisherman carefully guarding his secret formula for bait-making; wonderful and terrible are the smells which waft on the air when it is bait-making time at our house!

Jesus chose fishermen to be his friends, maybe because he knew the qualities of a fisherman, that stickability, dogged determination against all the odds, and their pride in their trade. They would need those self-same qualities as they learned the Master's art of winning men and women for the kingdom of God. They would make plenty of mistakes, but then, as I was told often enough when I was growing up, 'If you never make a mistake you will never make anything.'

Simon, Andrew, James and John – four fishermen who became great saints, great examples, who heard the call of Jesus and left their nets to go with him in his mission to the world. Jesus still calls ordinary men and women going about their daily lives to follow him. He still offers them the most glittering prize of all, of sharing his ministry, of winning men and women. What Oxbridge situation, or multinational company, could compete with such an invitation?

Lord Jesus,
Help me to follow your example of discipline,
that I may be prepared in heart and mind to
hear your call and share your love and life with
others.

15

Nothing by Halves
(1.21–45)

Jesus set out on his ministry with the power and authority of God. He was accompanied by that group of ordinary working men with whom he had chosen to share his ministry. Jesus, who was God and man, with all heaven at his disposal, voluntarily limited himself, sharing the divine plan with a bunch of men who were hardly the brightest or the best. Why did he not choose the top people, the best brains, the most respected, people of influence? Why not a 'Jesus think-tank'? He could easily have avoided the 'nitty-gritty', the irksome petty restrictions of daily life. He could have stepped completely outside the problems of body, mind and spirit that human beings, even the most talented, have to live with. Instead he chose, yes chose, to share his work with the likes of you and me – and he still does, for that matter.

'Meekness and majesty, oh what a mystery!' Jesus was not 'half-and-half', half God and half man, but totally God, totally man, and he totally held together the divine and human nature. So when he went out into the synagogue and taught, he was greeted with amazement and wonder. It was his authority that stood out. It was not the sort they were used to. The scribes, the experts in the law, had as their authority the standing of the schools they had attended, the fact that they had sat at the feet of the learned and famous. Their authority was based on a code of reference to tradition, to what had happened in the past, and who had said it, the various interpretations which over the years had become, in their eyes, almost Holy Writ. Jesus came with personal authority.

As William Barclay, in his commentary on Mark's Gospel, puts it: 'He spoke with utter independence. He cited no authorities, and quoted no experts. He spoke with the finality of the voice of God.' His was the authority not just to speak but to act. Right there in the synagogue, the heart of the establishment, Jesus drove out an evil spirit from a man. He ordered the spirit to leave him and it did. That must have left the rest of the people open-mouthed. You don't expect that sort of thing to happen during Morning Prayer do you? He would have been the talk of 'high table', and on every street corner too.

From there Jesus went out for a meal with friends, to the home of one of his team, just a quiet evening with friends, to relax, to be, within the family situation. When they arrived they found that Peter's mother-in-law, who would have been preparing the meal, was in bed, ill with a fever. Jesus went to her, took her hand, and helped her up. Just like that! Supper might have been slightly late that evening, but what a celebration it was! There was a need, and Jesus met it. He wasn't just at home in the synagogue, not merely concerned with the spectacular, but with the ordinary, everyday affairs of human life.

News travelled fast! Here was someone who cared, someone who could help, really help. People began flocking to him, bringing with them their friends who were in need, those sick in body, sick in mind. They didn't wait for morning, here was someone who could help *now* – and he did. The lovely old evening hymn describes this event:

> At even, when the sun was set,
> The sick, O Lord, around thee lay.
> O in what divers pains they met,
> O with what joy they went away!

17

Jesus did not confine himself to one place, to one situation. It was people who mattered, and so whether in the synagogue, in a private home or on the streets, he met them where they were, as they were. He was besieged by those who for the first time were given hope, real hope, by someone with real authority and genuine love.

Jesus must have had little sleep that night, but early in the morning he was up and out, to be with his Father, to be at one with him, to seek his guidance as to the next step. His peace was soon disturbed. His friends were looking for him – 'Jesus is a great success, stay with it!' Jesus knew, though, that he had to be on the move. There were others who needed to hear the good news of God. He was not concerned to gain a reputation for being a wonderful healer, but that people should come to know God. He healed out of love, an expression of the love and power of God. But that was but one part of his ministry.

Jesus' ministry was of preaching, teaching and healing – a message, a demonstration, of the wholeness of the gospel. It has not changed, and that ministry he has committed to his Church, his people. For centuries the healing ministry of the Church was neglected. Thank God it has now been rediscovered, and particularly in these last few years through the work of such people as Bishop Morris Maddocks, formerly Bishop of Selby, and Adviser for the Ministry of Health and Healing to the Archbishops of Canterbury and York. He writes in the Preface to his book, *The Christian Healing Ministry*: 'His renewed commission sends us out especially among the sick and the poor, the under-privileged and the hungry, the anxiety-ridden and the downtrodden, to proclaim the fact that Christ heals and saves . . .'

As we travel together through Mark's Gospel we shall see how Jesus changed lives and situations with authority, power and love. He reached out to a tormented man and freed him, he healed a friend's relative in her own home, he touched the 'untouchable', the leper, restoring to him not only his body, but his dignity, his life. No wonder everybody flocked to him. Wouldn't you?

Take a look at the world today, as it is. Look at your own community, the square mile around you. What do you see? I see people who need to know freedom and release. I see every kind of sickness and disease, not least the pressures of modern life with its uncertainties and tensions. I see ignorance and desperate, unfilled longing for something, or someone to bring help and hope. That old evening hymn has in its last verse these words:

> Thy touch has still its ancient power,
> No word from thee can fruitless fall.

But how are the people out there to know that, to hear that, to experience his touch on their lives? Only if those who know Jesus, who have experienced for themselves his release, his healing and loving touch, through his words, through 'signs and wonders', through being part of his body here on earth today, are willing to reach out in his name for him. People like you and me.

Lord Jesus,
Please reach out now and touch me. Forgive, restore, renew me and make me whole. Then enable me, by your grace and power, to reach out to others with the good news of your love.

19

What Matters Most?
(2.1–12)

We live in a world of instant communication. We see and hear the news as it happens, all due to sophisticated technology, a wonder of our modern life and time scale. Yet to my mind there is an even more amazing form of communication, what is known as 'bush telegraph' – news spread at enormous speed by word of mouth. Good news – and bad - travels fast without the aid of technology. Human interest is a powerful medium!

The news about Jesus spread like wildfire: 'Here is someone who heals the sick, instantaneously. This we must see!' So when Jesus went back to Capernaum where he had so powerfully preached and healed, the house where he was staying was packed inside and out. Everybody wanted to be there. The news that Jesus was in town was particularly good news for a group of friends, five of them to be exact. One of them was paralysed, dependent on the others to carry him around and look after him. It was a good job he had friends, for there were no social services, no health care or disability pension to help him. If you had family or friends who cared, then maybe you would be looked after, if not you begged or died. It was as simple as that. Sadly, that applies to vast parts of the world today as well.

Anyway, here was a chance in a lifetime, to take him along to meet Jesus. The four able-bodied friends hoisted the paralysed man, bed and all, on to their shoulders, and set off to find Jesus. Unfortunately, everybody else had the same idea, and no way could they get through the crowd. But it would take more than a crowd to deter them, so up on the flat-topped roof, and with their bare hands they made a space through the tiles and laths, just enough to get the bed through. Gently they lowered their friend down, so that he was right in front of Jesus.

There probably followed one of those breathless silences, as all eyes were fixed on the man. Then Jesus gently said to him, 'My son, your sins are forgiven.' No one said anything, but there was a great deal of thinking going on, and a great deal of criticism in the minds of the teachers of the law who had come along to find out what this preacher and healer was up to. Preaching and healing he might be able to do, but how dared he say he could forgive sins? 'What right has he? Only God can do that!' Jesus was quite aware of what they were thinking, and confronted them: 'Is it easier to say, "Your sins are forgiven", or "Take up your bed and walk"?' That was an easy question, for you can't see if sins have been forgiven, but you can certainly see if a person has been healed of a physical condition. Jesus had played into their hands – and then came the bombshell. 'I'll prove to you that the Son of Man has authority to forgive sins,' said Jesus – and to the man lying there, 'Get up, pick up your mat and go home.' And he did! He got up and walked away, forgiven and healed.

The crowd thought it was marvellous. Never before had they seen or heard anything like it – no wonder they praised God. The teachers, though, were furious. To them it was blasphemy, and they were more determined than ever to get rid of Jesus, and the sooner the better. What about the four friends who had used brute force to enable their sick friend to meet Jesus? They must have been, in today's language, 'over the moon'. Now there were five fit, able-bodied men, for the one who had been unable to help himself had been lifted up by the power of God's forgiveness, able to 'walk tall' in health of body and soul. He had been given his freedom. Now he could begin to live.

I did say that you cannot see if sins have been forgiven or not, but that is a very misleading statement. Feelings of guilt, unconfessed sin, fear of the consequences, can cause all sorts of problems ranging from vague aches and pains, depression and anxiety to chronic physical complaints. So many people are caught up in a personal conspiracy of silence so that they find it difficult to seek help; they are literally paralysed by it. We don't know what had happened in the life of that paralysed man before he met Jesus. We do know that as Jesus looked at him he recognised his deepest need, and met it. He was healed, made whole, and so could walk in freedom from all that had held him captive.

A friend of mind who is a doctor in general practice told me a long time ago, 'Many of the people who come into my surgery do not need a doctor, they need a minister.' It is true, I know, for I meet people through my work as a minister, and as a Christian writer and broadcaster, who are in great distress, desperately unhappy because for years they have carried a burden of sin and guilt, but felt they could never be forgiven and so had been unable to share it with anyone. I try, through prayer, counselling and by pointing them to the assurance in the Bible, to show them that there is forgiveness available; the past can be dealt with; they can be free.

The teachers of the law were correct when they said that only God could forgive sin. How terribly sad it was that when they saw a forgiven sinner they could not do what the ordinary folk around did, and praise God. What a tragedy that they were so spiritually paralysed by their own self-righteousness that they did not see their own need, nor recognise the power and love of the Son of God who stood before them. Jesus comes today as then to save, restore, heal and set men and women free from their sin. That was his purpose in coming to this earth, and it is still his purpose today. It is his purpose for you and for me, that we also may know the joy of being 'ransomed, healed, restored, forgiven' – and show it in our lives.

Lord Jesus,
Thank you that you have the power to forgive my sins. Thank you that in your love you do. May I hear your words of assurance, 'Your sins are forgiven,' and walk before you in newness of life from now on.

For Sinners Only

(2.13–17)

'Come round to my place for dinner. There's someone I'd like you to meet – I guarantee you have
never met anyone quite like him before. I've asked
a few of his friends along as well, and all our crowd
are coming . . .' An intriguing invitation! Levi had
something up his sleeve, or someone. There was
that preacher, Jesus, in the area; everybody seemed
to have either heard him or was going to hear him,
but 'I can't imagine he would be Levi's cup of tea.'
Levi had no time for religion, nor religion for him,
doing that job of tax collecting. Religion and tax
collecting don't go together somehow.

Religion, maybe not, but Jesus and tax collectors
certainly did. There was Levi – Matthew as we
know him – sitting in his office getting on with his
paper work, his mind on the job, when Jesus walked
up to him and said, 'Follow me'. – just like that. And
Levi put down his pen, closed the book, left the
office, and that was that. He had taken immediate
early retirement. Come to think of it, he wasn't of
retirement age, and tax collecting was a job for life,
and a pretty good one at that, in spite of all the
hassle. Levi gave it up – for what? One thing for sure,
no one else would give him a job now, not after what
he had been mixed up in, working for the Roman
government, taking money off his own people for
those invaders, *and* making plenty on the side for
his own pocket. He was clever all right, and no fool,
so why on earth had he done something so out of
character, joining the Jesus lot?

So there they were, round at Levi's place, enjoying
the meal and the company, Jesus and his disciples,

and Levi's friends, other tax collectors and rather dubious characters. Jesus didn't seem to be at all bothered that they were there. He looked as though he was enjoying their company, and they were certainly enjoying being with him. He wasn't shouting at them, telling them off or anything, in fact he was listening to what they had to say, very relaxed and friendly, even though they were not the sort of people you would think a man of God would mix with. He ought to be with the rabbis and the teachers. After all, they knew about God and all that.

Jesus, friend of sinners – and so he was. He didn't divide people into groups, or have a list of acceptable and non-acceptable acquaintances. He was willing to get alongside anyone, anywhere, any time. His invitation was for anyone who would take it up – as Levi had. It didn't matter where you had come from, it was where you were going that mattered – and Levi was going with Jesus, and wanted his friends to have the chance to decide for themselves about Jesus too.

Levi wanted to share his friends with Jesus. He wasn't ashamed of his friends, nor was he ashamed of the decision he had made to change his lifestyle. So what better way than to invite them all around for dinner, to let them get acquainted – and it was going fine . . . until those law teachers happened to come by and see what was going on. They called over the disciples of Jesus and in a rather snide way wanted to know what Jesus was doing eating with these people. These were not the sort of people they would be seen with, and if Jesus was, as he said, from God, then what was he doing here? 'Doesn't he know what sort of people they are?' Surely Jesus had some code of behaviour, some standards?

That was two thousand years ago, but the same sort of accusations and questionings still go on as people look at the friends of Jesus, those who go to church, who share at his table. 'Just a bunch of hypocrites . . . a load of sinners . . . Call themselves Christians, do you know what he did? . . . what she was up to? . . . They want to get their lives straightened out before they start going on about Jesus. . .'

Yes, it is true, the Church is full of all sorts of people, sinners true enough, like me, I know that. I know the promises I make and fail miserably to keep, my bad temper, my impatience. I know well enough, and I have enough people who draw my attention to them frequently – which doesn't always help my temper either! Being a minister in a small church in a small town means a rather goldfish-like existence; nothing escapes attention, particularly what I am doing, saying or looking like! And that goes for all those who dare to call themselves the friends of Jesus. The wonderful thing is, though, Jesus offers his friendship and his love to sustain us day by day. It doesn't matter what others think about us, whether they consider we are beyond the pale or not, whether they can point their fingers at our shortcomings and failures. What matters is that Jesus loves us, and is not ashamed to be called our friend. He understands us, knows our weaknesses, and will help us. Jesus' answer to the remarks about the company he kept was, 'People who are well do not need a doctor, but only those who are sick. I have not come to call respectable people, but outcasts.'

'Respectable people' – or those who *think* they are respectable – good, religious, praiseworthy people. Sadly they are satisfied with their lives, their own power, their own goodness, and so see no need for Jesus, see no need to associate with those of his friends whose lives seem so inadequate and who admit they are not what they should be.

Back to Levi – Matthew. A tax collector, a sinner, an outcast from his own people, but Jesus called him, and wanted him for a friend. The friendship of Jesus transformed Matthew into the great Christian apostle, Gospel writer, saint. So what has all this to say to us today? I well remember an old chorus I learned just after I became a Christian:

It is no secret what God can do.
What he's done for others he'll do for you.
With arms wide open, he'll welcome you.
It is no secret what God can do.

No secret indeed, for Jesus is the friend of sinners – and always will be!

Lord,
May I never consider anyone to be beyond your friendship, or outside your love, nor sit in judgement on another person's life. Jesus, friend of sinners, be my friend, for I need you most of all.

Come and Join the Celebration

(2.18–28)

When Peter and I got married back in 1960 our wedding followed the traditional pattern: late morning wedding followed by 'wedding breakfast' – or rather lunch in our case – then off we went on honeymoon to Anglesey, arriving there in good time for supper. Nowadays couples often opt for a formal family lunch following the ceremony and a disco at night for their young friends. The bride and bridegroom 'dance the night away' before catching their flight next day for some far-flung, exotic location. It is all very different from a Jewish wedding in the time of Jesus. Then the bride and bridegroom did not go away on honeymoon, but spent it at home. It was 'open house' for a week of continual celebration, eating, drinking, talking, dancing, a grand reunion for the families and friends from near and far – a 'holiday of a lifetime', for a wedding was the high spot of anyone's life. Day-to-day living was hard and tough going for everyone, with no time, or energy, or wherewithal to have parties, so when the chance came they made the most of it. The honeymoon was enjoyed by everyone. The harsh realities of life would come soon enough, so on with the feasting!

Jesus used the illustration of a wedding when confronted with the question of fasting. John the Baptist's followers fasted, as did the very religious followers of the Pharisees; it was a sign of their godliness, their dedication. So why didn't the disciples of Jesus fast like they did? Jesus wanted to show them that life with him was a joyous thing, it was like a honeymoon period, meant to be enjoyed

28

to the full. The time would soon come when they would weep, and fast, and be sad (Jesus was hinting at the time when he would be taken from his friends, but that was in the future). For now, life was to be enjoyed, not endured.

Jesus revelled in the company of his friends, he delighted to share with them, to be able to teach them new things, to open their eyes to the wonder of God's love. He was the new coat, the new wineskin. He hadn't come to patch up life, to 'make do and mend', but to make all things new by the extravagance of his love. That was to cost him everything, even his life. It was the same with the Sabbath. What had been given by God as a gift, a joy, had been hedged about by so many rules and regulations, so many man-made obligations, that it had become a chore, a burden to be borne rather than a delight and pleasure.

Jesus was not saying there was no need for a time of fasting and self denial, that God's law could be flouted, or ignored, but he was pointing to the spirit of the law rather than the letter, which had been overwritten so many times that the original had almost been obliterated. An obsession with keeping rules and regulations may not be the mark of our life today – rather a throwing off of restraints, traditions and obligations – but what have we put in their place? Jesus offered a new way of life. For many, he has been discarded along with everything else and all that is left is a spirit of anarchy, and an aching void which sees no rhyme or reason to life.

One of the great sadnesses I personally feel is the loss of Sunday. It has been gradually eroded away, until we are left with a day like any other day of the week when people rush frantically around, getting nowhere fast. A backlash against the Victorian

Sunday, maybe, but the God-given gift of a day of rest was intended for our good, body, mind and spirit. The human frame cannot go on day after day, week after week, without regular breaks, a release from work and routine. The mind cannot continue to cope with the burdens we place on it, while the spiritual side shrivels, dies, and the wholeness of life that God intended for us is put out of joint, and deformed, and we all suffer. I look forward to Sunday. It is for me a heaven-sent opportunity to share with others, to have time to spend in God's house and with his people, to be free from the demands of the week, to be able to relax, to breathe, to be. There is also the bonus of going into town without the crowds of shoppers, the fumes of commercial vehicles, the hurried pace of life. Sunday should be a fun-day in the real sense of the word. How sad it is that we load ourselves with unnecessary burdens, we add our own rules and regulations, and wonder why we collapse under the strain. Even in our Christian life we so easily become legalistic. Jesus is Lord of our life, so let us enjoy him! What we do should be done out of love for him, an expression of our praise and thankfulness, and a loving recognition of the needs of our brothers and sisters around us.

A little lad came up to me very proudly the other day, beaming from ear to ear. 'Mrs Cundiff, I've got a new anorak – look – it's new, my dad bought it me – it hasn't been anybody else's.' I knew what he was talking about. He is the youngest of a big family, and tends to get 'hand-me-downs', and even though he is always well dressed it had given him a special thrill to have something that was bought just for him. That little lad is special, he is a one-off, not just one of a family, and his dad was proving it to him. It was more than just an anorak, it was a token of the special bond between them. And it is the same with God and us.

We are not meant to force ourselves, or be forced, into an outworn, patched-up religious overall, but to enjoy the new life Jesus has given us, the new clothing of faith. We are meant to see life as a celebration, the new wine, today's 'special offer', in a container fitting for such an occasion, and to show to the world what it means to belong to Jesus Christ. We don't need to apologise for Jesus, or to be ashamed of what he has given us. Nor should we be brow-beaten by the world's attitude to his special day of the week. After all, it is the great celebration day, the reminder of his rising from the dead. It should be as joyful and exciting as any wedding feast, for it is a feast, and we are all his special guests. 'The Lord says, Come.' – What are we waiting for?

Lord,
Thank you for providing all the ingredients we need to make life a daily celebration of love. May we fashion our lives to your pattern, and show them to your praise and glory.

A Conflict of Opinion
(3.1–19, 22–30)

It was one of those special services for children, and
I had been invited along to preach. Knowing the
limited attention span of youngsters, I decided to
make the sermon spot more a conversation piece
than a monologue. 'What sort of person was Jesus?'
I asked them. Lots of hands went up: 'loving, gentle, good, kind, patient . . .' I nodded in agreement.
'That's right, he was. Do you think he ever got
really cross, shouted at people, knocked things
over, argued with them?' The children looked
doubtful; they were obviously thinking it was a
trick question! 'Well then, did he enjoy a good
night out, having fun, going to parties, did he tell
jokes?' No one was going to commit themself so
they waited for someone else to give them a clue.
'Well, what do you think Jesus looked like?' A hand
shot up. 'Like that, Mrs Cundiff,' said the lad –
pointing to the stained glass window. Yes, there
was Jesus, surrounded by angels and sheep, his eyes
turned to heaven. Tall, thin, gloomy-looking, and
in case there should be any problem as to identi-
fication he had a halo round his head. He looked as
though a breath of wind would blow him over, and
the description that came to mind was a very modern one – he looked 'a wimp'.

Sadly so much stained glass, religious art and the
older type of religious books give that impression,
the 'gentle Jesus, meek and mild' image, which
does not reflect the full picture of the Jesus of the
Gospels. I explained to the children that yes, Jesus
was good and kind and loving, but he also got very
cross with some people. It made him angry when

32

people took advantage of others, and he told them so and showed them so. He was also great company, loved to have people around, enjoyed his meals, and was the greatest story-teller. He was also very strong, after all, he was a carpenter, used to working hard. He was at ease talking to anyone, but he could also discuss and argue with the finest brains of his day. Above all, he was a man of great courage and determination. Certainly he could not be described as 'a wimp'!

We see Jesus being angry in this chapter. It's the Sabbath day, the day set aside for worship, and Jesus comes to the synagogue. There's a man there with a paralysed hand. There are also people there, Pharisees in particular, who are looking for evidence to convict Jesus of breaking the religious laws – so if Jesus heals the man, that is working on the Sabbath, and they have a case. Jesus pre-empts their case by asking them a question: 'What does our law allow us to do, save a man's life or destroy it?' They know the answer all right, but they are speechless, they will not admit Jesus is right. Jesus is angry with them because they are so stubborn even when they know they are wrong; and yet at the same time he feels sorry for them, because their stubbornness is depriving them of sharing in the joy of seeing God at work. Sadly, Jesus' act of compassion in healing the man was not seen as evidence of God's love and care, but of his breaking man-made rules and regulations which they considered essential to acceptance by God. The arguments they used against Jesus were so weak, and they must have known how flawed they were, and yet they persisted in their stubbornness. They could not deny his power, it was so evident, but they accused him of being in league with the devil, of being mad, anything but acknowledge the truth.

There is a popular expression, 'Case weak, shout harder' – certainly a good description of the case against Jesus. Not only did they shout harder, but they incited others to shout with them; and sadly the opposition to Jesus did harden, gathering strength with their friends in high places, and through the desire for political expediency.

Yet the ordinary people flocked to Jesus. They were not interested in academic argument, they could not understand the political and ecclesiastical manoeuvring. What they did know was that here was someone who could help them, who cared about them, who did not keep them at arms' length but touched them, held them, was one of them. He identified with them and they knew he was real.

It is said that Jesus had a bias to the poor, and in many ways of course he had, and to the under-privileged, the rejected and outcasts of society. But the good news he came to bring was for everyone. He did not divide people into classes, or groups, or nationalities. He did not look at their backgrounds, their bank balances, or their standing in the community, their intelligence quotients or their physical attributes, he just saw people in need. Those who recognised their need and were open to Jesus and what he could do in their lives became rich in heaven's currency. Those who were stubborn, self-centred and hard, chose by their own doing to remain in their poverty, spiritually bankrupt. The twelve men whom Jesus called to be his disciples were a very mixed bag – some fishermen, a tax collector, a 'freedom fighter', with working class, lower class and socially outcast amongst them. Stuart Blanch in his book *Encounters with Jesus* says of them that: 'The twelve disciples, later to be apostles, did not owe their place in the Church to their natural virtues, or their natural strength, but

34

to the fact they had been called, and had obeyed. That is what discipleship means – everywhere, and at all times.'

The invitation to know Jesus, to be his friend and follower, to enjoy his companionship, his way of life, here on earth and for all eternity, is not a privilege extended to the favoured few, but to all of us. No qualifications are needed, just an open heart and willing obedience; he will provide everything else. It all sounds so simple – too simple for those who want to cross the t's and dot the i's, have all the small print embodied in legal niceties, 'signed, sealed and delivered'. But for those who will trust him, Jesus offers freedom, life, adventure and a sure hope.

Simple? Yes it is. But a word of caution – it is not easy, he does not promise it will be, but he does promise that he will be with us – always. That, to my mind, makes it an offer I cannot refuse!

Lord,
You know me. I am so set in my ways at times. I am stubborn, self-centred and so sure I know it all.
I must make you angry at times. Yet you love me, you are sorry for me, you want to give me so much.
Give me the grace to admit when I am wrong, to turn from my self and accept your love, your way, your will, today and always.

Family Ties
(3.20, 21, 31–33)

Although Jesus lived here on earth for thirty-three years, almost all we know about him happened during his last three years, the span of his public ministry. Matthew and Luke in their Gospel accounts give us details of his human ancestry, of the visit of the angel Gabriel to Mary telling her she was to 'have a baby by the Holy Spirit', and of the confirmation of this to Joseph in a dream. We have the details of his birth, brief reference to the time in Egypt and their return to Nazareth, where it would seem Joseph followed his trade as a carpenter and they were a devout orthodox family, making their yearly visit to Jerusalem for the Passover festival.

It was when Jesus was twelve years old, during that annual visit, that we have another picture of him, recorded in Luke 2.41–52. Evidently all had gone as normal during the Passover festival and they were on their way home, in company with family and friends – the equivalent of today's 'group travel' – and it was not until they had gone a full day's journey that it was realised Jesus was missing. Mary and Joseph were desperately anxious, and there was nothing for it but to go back to Jerusalem to see if he was there. Fearing the worst they scoured the city. On the third day, by which time they must have been frantic with worry, they found Jesus in the Temple, conversing with the teachers, listening to all that was going on, and making a very adult and authoritative contribution. We can well imagine how his parents were so wound up, at their wits' end, and there he was without a thought for all the trouble and distress he had caused. When asked why he had done this his answer sounds very precocious: 'Didn't you know that I had to be in my Father's house?' I have to be honest, if I had been his mother I would have given him a clip round the ear, and kept him in for weeks afterwards! We are not told any more about the incident except that they went back home, Jesus did as he was told and 'grew both in body and wisdom, gaining favour with God and men'. Mary, his mother, we are told 'treasured all these things in her heart', and we are privileged to have had recorded for us his mother's response.

So what happened between the ages of twelve and thirty? Jesus settled down, followed in Joseph's footsteps, became a carpenter. Evidently he turned out to be the sort of son any parent would be proud of, liked by everyone, hard working, active in the local synagogue. Yes, he was a credit to his family and his upbringing, a thoroughly nice young man, obviously destined to be a pillar of local society. Today, no doubt, he would have been an Elder in the church, or a PCC member, perhaps a local Parish Councillor with the possibility of becoming a magistrate in a few years' time.

Then when it all seemed so safe and predictable, he left home, went off and got involved with John the Baptist, was baptised by him in the Jordan, and set up on his own as a travelling preacher with a group of followers. Reports began coming through that he was attracting a great deal of attention, not just by his preaching but by performing miracles, healing the sick and driving out demons. The religious authorities were not very happy about the sort of things he was doing and saying, and in fact some of them said he was mad, and he should be stopped.

Mary and Joseph and the family must have been desperately unhappy about all of this. After all, look what had happend to John the Baptist. He had upset the authorities and in no time at all had been imprisoned and then executed. If Jesus wasn't careful the same was likely to happen to him. There were some very ominous mutterings going on. Jesus was getting far too popular with the ordinary people, and the religious and political leaders were not going to stand for that; he spelled trouble, and needed nipping in the bud, preferably for ever.

There was only one thing to do, the family decided. They would go and bring him home, get him to settle down again, to keep quiet, to stop all this running round the country attracting attention. He had to be stopped, for his own good.

The problem was how to get to him. When Mary and some of the family arrived at the house where Jesus was staying there was no way they could get through the crowd to talk to him on their own. So they sent in a message; they wanted to have a word with him – in private. The message was delivered all right, the little family group on the edge of the crowd were pointed out to Jesus: 'Look, your mother and your brothers and sisters are outside and want you.' Surely his first obligation was to go to them at once. They were family, they had a claim on him. If he was a good religious man, then he would obey God's commandment to 'honour your father and your mother'. Instead, Jesus ignored the request, and speaking directly to the crowd gathered round him, told them *they* were his family, and that whoever does what God wants them to do was his brother, his sister or his mother.

Jesus' treatment of his family, when they had shown such concern for him, seems rude, unloving and unkind. Yet he had to show them that he had to put God's will and work first, even before family. If he had given in to their demands, then his ministry would have been ruined. 'Look,' his critics would have said, 'he has had to see sense, so they've taken him away now. He knew he was in the wrong.' Jesus was part of a human family, but he had come to show the world that being part of God's family is more important than anything else. He came to bring people into a relationship with God as their Father, to be 'born again' and therefore into a new relationship with each other as brothers and sisters as well.

Sometimes in life very painful decisions have to be made which involve saying 'no' to family for the sake of saying 'yes' to God. I am so thankful that my parents never stood in my way as I followed what I believed was God's will for my life. I do know they took a lot of criticism for it. There were those who said to them, 'You want to watch that daughter of yours, going so religious.' I am sure that at times they did not understand why I was following the path I did, but they went on loving and supporting me regardless, and I praise God for them. But I have met many who have not received the same support and understanding, men and women who had to give up everything, were cut off from their families because of their faith, and it is still happening. I am sure their parents' motives are good. They want to protect their children, want what they think is 'the best' for them. It causes great heartache on both sides, I know that, but at the end of the day each human being has to follow their own calling, and that must be respected. I once saw a poster with these words: 'There are two gifts you can give to your children, roots and wings'. As a mother myself, I know the truth of that. Bringing up children is not easy, in fact it is hard work, but it is a labour of love, and you try to give them a safe, secure and loving base for life.

Then, having seen them rooted in love, you have to allow them to fly, whether to the next street or across the world, to 'follow in father's footsteps' or to do something entirely different. It is their life, not ours.

Jesus could not allow anyone to stand in the way of his Father's will for him. He had to take the risk of hurting his family, upsetting the authorities, confusing his friends. In the end it cost him his life. No easy decision, was it? What of his family? We know that Mary his mother stood by him, even at the cross. He gave her into the loving care of his friend John, who took her and cared for her as his own mother, and she cared for him as a son. Jesus' brother James became head of the Church in Jerusalem, and another brother, Jude, succeeded him, so some of the family did come to understand, to realise the truth of his calling and to respond to him by faith, not just as their son or their brother, but as Saviour and Lord, and to be brought into the biggest family in the world – the one which you and I also are part of, through faith in him.

Heavenly Father,
Thank you for those who have the courage and
dedication to put your will above all other con-
siderations, even of family ties. Grant to their
families and friends your grace and gift of loving
acceptance, even when they cannot understand,
and may they finally know the joy of being all
one in Jesus, and part of your family on earth
and in heaven.

Spread the Word
(4.1–20)

I came into the wonderful world of communications in the mid-Seventies when I was appointed Broadcasting Officer in the Diocese of York, part of the official Communications Department. It was a wonderful world indeed, not least for being part of a network of 'Communication Officers' in the Church of England. I suppose over the years we have looked at the word 'communication' from every possible angle. I have been to umpteen conferences, a multitude of meetings, and read almost every book on the subject, as my bookshelf reminds me, from the 'nuts and bolts' of writing press releases and scripts, to the study of the theology of communications, the art of public speaking and technical information. It is all there on my shelf, and hopefully in my head and my fingers too! What has helped me most, though, has been meeting and listening to people who are good communicators, those practitioners who have the great gift of instant communication. They hold my attention throughout, and imprint their message on the heart and in the mind in such a way that it remains, and can be recalled. It is both an art and a science, but most of all it is a gift, and I listen to the great ones with awe and admiration.

But the number one communicator of all time is Jesus. As I look at him I see what it is all about. Here he was, surrounded by a noisy crowd. How could he make himself heard, even by those at the back? He got into a boat, had it pushed out a little way, creating a natural theatre and auditory system – no need for a microphone or seating plan.

41

So much for the mechanics, how about the message? How to convey concepts and ideas to ordinary people who were unused to debate and argument? So he told them stories – parables, the definition of which I learned in Sunday school as 'an earthly story with a heavenly meaning'. Those stories have remained superb examples of how to convey eternal truths on so many different levels; and the Parable of the Sower is just one of them.

'Listen. Once there was a man who went out to sow corn . . .' Of course they were listening. They all knew what Jesus was talking about, it was part of their own experience. As he spoke they could probably see a man over in the fields doing just that, sowing his seeds, striding up and down, broadcasting the seed to the left and to the right, his hands moving rhythmically in tune with his pace. As he sowed, some of the seed fell on the path, on the rocky outcrops, on ground which already had thorns and thistles established below the surface and which would choke the seeds as they germinated and began to expand. Poor ground, yes, some of it was – but that was only part of the story. There was also good ground, well prepared, which brought a good return. The sower did not waste his seed or his time, he knew from experience that his was the best way of sowing, in spite of the 'natural wastage', and at the end of the day the harvest was sure.

You could call it 'an everyday story of country folk', telling it how it was. Those who heard Jesus knew he was describing the process perfectly. So what then? 'Listen, then, if you have ears!' For the most part they had heard enough, they had homes to go to, work to be done, people to see, they would listen to Jesus later. But there were some who realised that there was more to the story than a reminder of agricultural practice, and they joined the disciples clustering around Jesus, a small group of friends rather than an audience.

You probably know as well as I do the explanation Jesus gave those who were prepared to listen to it. The sower has the most valuable seed in all the world, God's life-giving word. It is freely sown, extravagantly scattered upon the human race; whether it takes root depends upon its reception. There are those who are totally indifferent to the goods news; there is not even a crack or a chink where it might even lodge; it is immediately lost, it hasn't a chance. Some, like rocky soil, happily receive it; the word is alive, but it has no chance to take hold, nothing to sustain it, like a plant which is given neither water nor light, which is never fed or cared for. A promising beginning, but with no support to bring the word to be of any use. Then again, the precious seed is received happily, in fertile conditions, with plenty of room for growth for a healthy plant, but there are other things demanding space, and intent on taking over, things like worries, ambition, successes, opportunities to advance in the world, to make a name and a profit. These things can put a stranglehold on the development of a spiritual life. Oh yes, the plant will grow, and come into flower, there may even be signs of a seed head, but eventually it is overpowered and overclouded by the concerns of this life: 'I haven't got time,' 'I'm too busy,' 'I just can't think straight at the moment,' 'I've got to get this job sorted out,' – strong, powerful and dangerous excuses for neglecting the spiritual life.

It is only when we are open and prepared to hear and receive God's word and give it room to grow and develop, when we are willing to get rid of the things which would hinder the growth, and are not only willing but actively get to grips with doing so, that what God has sown in our hearts and lives will come to fruition, and will fulfil its useful purpose. After all, the sower sows to get results. He looks for and expects a harvest. God looks for results in our lives too!

As I look at my life I see areas of hardness, of shallow 'promises, promises' which never get anywhere, areas of preoccupation with my own life, with what I want to to do, what I want to be. I allow these things to put a stranglehold on my effective ministry, and it's often not until I feel the life being squeezed from me that I come to my senses. It is often a very painful process, and could have been avoided if I had taken more care.

The joy is, though, that the sower does not sow once, but over and over again, year in year out. He never gives up, because he is confident of a harvest. In the book of Isaiah there is a promise which I hold on to, and it is this: 'My word is like the snow and the rain that come down from the sky to water the earth . . . So also will be the word that I speak – it will not fail to do what I plan for it; it will do everything I send it to do' (Isaiah 55.10–11).

God does not give up on me or you; we get chance after chance after chance. But how sad that we waste those chances so often, when we could have been beautiful and useful if only we had listened and received what he had for us. Take heart, though. Jesus says, 'Listen, then, if you have ears.' Let's pray now that we may do so.

Lord,
Thank you for your patience in spelling out in ways we can understand, your eternal truths. May we be quick to hear and ready to receive all you have to give to us, and produce in our lives the result you look for and will delight in.

Why are You Afraid?

(4.21–41)

One of my favourite old hymns, 'Tell me the old, old story' has a verse which runs like this,

Tell me the story often, for I forget so soon.
The early dew of morning has passed away at noon.

I always sing that with great conviction and not a little shame, but I know it to be true of me, and I suspect for most other people. Take the disciples for instance. They were in a very privileged position, unique in fact. Front-row observers of all Jesus said and did, they could listen to all those wonderful stories and parables Jesus told – those vivid picture-stories of lamps under beds or on lampstands; of farmers sowing seeds and the way the harvest comes to fruition, of the mustard seed, that tiny seed which when full grown is one of the biggest of all plants. Ordinary, everyday things, pointing to great truths about man and God; parables of the kingdom of heaven. The crowds delighted in the stories, and some grasped something of what Jesus was really talking about, but the disciples had the benefit of personal tuition, for when the crowd drifted away then Jesus explained the deep significance of those stories. They were being trained, prepared for what lay ahead, so that they would not panic but have the foundation of teaching to understand the situations they would be thrown into. Sharing in the ministry of Jesus so closely, they were given 'hands on' experience that would build their confidence and trust in him for all times.

45

They were soon to be put to the test, in trial by water, and very stormy water at that! They had all had such a busy and tiring time, and needed a break. Jesus needed peace and quiet, and to relax with his friends. It was no use staying where they were, the answer was to go across the lake away from the crowds. They had a boat, and they were experienced in handling it; after all, at least four of the disciples were professional fishermen, and they all knew the lake, there was no problem. Then suddenly a storm blew up, something that was quite common, for the Lake of Galilee was and is noted for sudden storms. So, nothing new, but this was a particularly bad storm, so bad that the boat was almost submerged, rapidly filling with water, and even those experienced fishermen knew what that meant, they were in imminent danger of drowning.

Yet what was Jesus doing? He was sound asleep, quite oblivious, or so they thought, of what was happening to them. Desperately they went to him and woke him. They were frightened to death, and in accusing tone yelled, 'Teacher, don't you care we are about to die?' How could Jesus sleep at such a time? Surely he should be helping them. After all, they were his best friends, entitled to his help. Jesus stood up. 'Be still,' he said to the wind. 'Be still,' he said to the sea, and then he silenced his disciples. 'Why are you frightened? Have you still no faith?'

The sea was calm now, the wind was stilled, but their hearts must have been thumping. They were frightened. They had witnessed the awesome power of Jesus not only to hold the hearts of men and women by his teaching and preaching, to minister forgiveness, healing and release, but also to control the elements. The words of Jesus must have cut them: 'Have you *still* no faith?' After all the time and effort, all his love and patience, in an emergency they were not better than anyone else, behaving like frightened children. Jesus must have been saddened. Would these men ever grow up? Would the message ever penetrate their hearts and minds and lives? They would have to face worse than physical storms before very long. How would they cope?

I meet many Christians who sadly have never got beyond the 'listening to stories' stage in their Christian lives. They have their favourite passages of Scripture, and will come to services and meetings as long as they are not too demanding. They complain if the service goes on an extra five minutes, or the passage of Scripture is an unfamiliar one. Really, they want to be entertained, to be made to feel 'happy', and their frequent complaint is, 'I didn't get anything out of it.' They are still part of the crowd scene.

Yet others want to go deeper. They are prepared to study, to 'dig deep'. They want to learn more, to understand what the Christian faith is all about, and in doing so discover that God's power is at work in the world, in the lives of people around them today just as much as when Jesus was present in the flesh. Then something happens that hits them for six, maybe an illness, a tragedy, or some emergency, and they feel they are going under, and there is no one to help them. Then God gets the blame. 'Don't you care about me? If you did care you'd help me.' The accusations come thick and fast, and there are those who go under, because they are looking only at the problem rather than to Jesus. They forget what they have learned, what they have heard, and what they have experienced of the love and power of God.

None of us will go through life without meeting the unexpected, feeling at times that we are going under, having to cope with the storms of life. But if we will day by day seek to know the Lord better, and keep close to him, then, like the man who 'built his house on the rock', we can know the peace and calm in the storm, in the crisis, in the tragedy.

Maybe sometimes it does feel as though Jesus is far away, that he has gone to sleep and we are scared stiff. I know I am. Yet I think of people I know who have gone through the most dreadful experiences, one thing after another, and yet know the peace of the Lord, and show it. I am put to shame by them many, many times. An elderly lady in our church, Hannah, has gone completely blind, but there is never a word of anger or fear. 'The Lord is good,' is a phrase constantly on her lips, and shown in her life. Always encouraging others, she is a bringer of peace and joy to all she meets. In her physical blindness she sees more and has a much clearer vision of the Lord than most of us who can read the small print on the optician's chart. Call it faith, call it trust, call it what you will, the peace of the Lord is always with her, and radiates out from her.

'Be quiet,' commanded Jesus to the wind and the waves, and they were. The psalmist could write, 'God is our shelter and strength, always ready to help in times of trouble. So we will not be afraid, even if the earth is shaken, and mountains fall into the ocean depths; even if the seas roar and rage . . .' (Psalm 46.1–3). And the command of God comes loud and clear to you and me just as it has to men and women through all time, 'Be still and *know* that I am God' (verse 10, RSV). It is as we respond to his command that we find our peace and our salvation, the assurance of making harbour at our final destination, with him, forever.

Lord,
When the storms of life blow up and I am so
afraid, remind me that you are with me, and
you will help me. Still my restless heart and
mind, that I may know your peace, your power
and your love.

Freed – at a Price
(5.1–20)

The disciples must have heaved a sigh of relief as they brought the boat to shore. They had been through a traumatic time, with the storm and the subsequent stilling of it by Jesus. They would have been in need of a rest, a time of quiet with Jesus alone, a break from noise, activity, demanding people and situations. It was not to be. As they came to shore, a frightening figure rushed towards them, a madman, so strong even chains could not hold him secure. He dashed wildly around, bent on destroying everything, himself included. When he saw Jesus he started screaming and shouting even louder, for he was possessed, not by one but by many evil spirits. And as Jesus had calmed the angry sea and the disciples' fears, he calmed the man by ordering the spirits to leave him and go into the herd of pigs nearby. At once the man was released, his sanity restored – but the herd of pigs went rushing madly down the cliff and were all drowned.

To us in the so-called 'modern' world, it may all sound rather bizarre and primitive. After all people today do not believe in evil spirits – or do we? It must be evident as we read our newspapers, listen to the radio or watch television, that evil spirits are still powerfully at large in the world today, whatever we call them. 'Something evil had got into her.' 'He was like a man possessed,' 'The place was charged with an awesome malevolent power,' – just three quotations from newspaper reports I read this week, and not in the more sensational press, but in what we call the 'quality newspapers'. There are still many people who have to be restrained from violence, both to themselves and others; and looking at the world scene, are there not those who we have to admit are controlled by devilish powers, and wreak destruction and misery on millions? Maybe this is something we would rather not think about, yet we cannot ignore the evidence before our eyes. We need to remember, too, that Jesus commissioned his followers to cast out demons, and that commission has never been rescinded. There is no doubt either that by the power of Jesus people are released from the evil that possessed them; it is not as unusual as we might have thought. A word of warning though: evil spirits are powerful, not to be played with or thought of lightly. There are in the Church trained, experienced counsellors and exorcists whose advice can be sought. We should never, never dabble!

Back to the man who had been released. It was wonderful news for him, but what about those pigs? It was bad news for those who were charged with looking after them, disaster for the owner whose livelihood they were. Why did Jesus do it this way? Surely he did it for the man who needed to see visibly and unmistakably that the devils had gone out of his life forever.

So everyone came rushing to see what had happened, not least those whose income had been tied up in the pigs. They were frightened to death by Jesus. What would he do next? The fact that a man had been given his sanity back was of no concern to them, it was the pigs they were worried about. The power that Jesus had to change lives and situations was too much for them. They preferred their lives as they were, and so they told Jesus to go. He disturbed their way of life, their way of thinking, and they could not cope with him.

The power of Jesus still disturbs people. Some would rather not know. After all, if Jesus stays around, maybe they will have to change their views, their habits, and even their livelihood. So they tell him to go away, they don't want to know him . . . and he goes. Jesus never forces himself upon anyone. The choice in the end is up to the individual. A disturbed life or a quiet life, which do you want? His way or yours? There is always a cost in following Jesus, a cost in being part of his Church; but then think of the cost to him to release us from sin and death – it cost him not his livelihood but his life, every last drop of it.

What of the man who had been the cause of all this disturbance? He was so overwhelmed with joy and gratitude, he wanted to stay with Jesus for ever. But Jesus says No. 'Go back home to your family and tell them how much the Lord has done for you, and how kind he has been to you' (verse 19). He was given the task which only he could do, to be a missionary, a witness to his own people of the power and the love of Jesus. 'Go and tell' – and he did. What a powerful testimony! I am sure he never tired of sharing the good news – and who knows how many came to faith because of his witness?

Perhaps this is something we need to ask ourselves: 'Do I share with my family and friends what the Lord has done for me, how kind he has been to me?' Have you got anything to share? And if you have, what are you doing about it?

Lord Jesus,
You were willing to give your life so I might be
set free.
As I rejoice in my freedom, may I always be ready
and willing to share the good news of your love
and power with others, wherever you send me.

Faith to Believe
(5.21–43)

On opposite pages of the newspaper were two photographs, a world apart. One showed a famous and extremely wealthy rock guitarist, holding his beautiful four-year-old son. They looked radiantly happy together, and why not? They were both handsome and healthy, and clearly loved one another dearly. That child would never lack for anything in life, for his father had both the love and the means to provide for him. A perfect picture of security, love and affection and the promise of a golden future.

The other picture contained many faces. I tried counting them but had to give up, there were so many. In the foreground was a man, bowed, weeping, carrying a small bundle which was his dead son. Despair and hopelessness were etched on every face in that photograph – it was common to them all, the badge of suffering. They had nothing, no future. Many of those in that photograph were probably dead already, I thought, even though it had been taken only two days before. They were refugees, frightened, homeless, starving and stateless. There are millions like them in the world.

The first photograph had also been taken quite recently, but the caption underneath spoke of an even more recent event, a few days before, when that child tragically fell to his death from a window accidentally left open. The caption read 'Despair!' Maybe those two photographs showed worlds apart, but they also reflected the fact that suffering, pain and death are common factors. Two fathers, both grieving for their dead sons, experienced the same emotions, the same loss. Their suffering was identical. What did it matter to them whether they were rich and famous or poor and unknown; what mattered was that they had lost their sons. Both were in the same boat. Sometimes great surprise is expressed when, for example, a beautiful actress contracts a serious disease, a famous figure experiences a tragic loss, or one of the 'top people' has family problems – as though they should be immune from these things, unlike ordinary people. It is said that 'money can't buy you love', and there are a lot of other things money can't buy, including health, happiness or a guaranteed life span. Some people may hit the newspaper headlines, others are part of an unknown crowd, but in the end they stand exactly the same in their need.

Two people worlds apart and both in need came to Jesus. We are told the name and position of one. Jairus is an important man at the local synagogue, happy and successful, with a lovely twelve-year-old daughter, obviously the joy of his life. Then she is taken desperately ill, and Jairus rushes to Jesus. Throwing himself at his feet he pleads for help. What does his position matter, or what people might think of him for going to this travelling preacher and healer? Jairus believes that Jesus can help his daughter, and to his joy and relief, Jesus sets off home with him. But the pace is so slow. There are so many people around. Jairus is getting more and more anxious by the minute. 'If only the people would leave him alone so we could get home quicker,' he must be thinking.

Unknown to Jairus, unknown to Jesus and unknown to anyone, in that crowd there is another desperate person. We are not told her name, only her complaint, an incurable haemorrhage. She has been ill for twelve years with it, has spent all her money trying to find a cure, with no success, getting worse instead of better; and besides that, it is regarded as an 'unclean' illness, so she is virtually a social outcast as well. She would not dare to draw attention to herself, by speaking to Jesus, but she has the faith that if she just touches his clothes she will be healed, she is sure of it. And so quietly, unobtrusively, she gets close to Jesus. Then, seeing her chance, she reaches out and touches him, and she knows in that instant she has been healed. As she slides away, Jesus stops and asks who it is who has touched him. A seemingly silly question – so many people are touching him. But this is different. He knows it is no accident, but an act of faith, a cry for help to him. The woman is petrified. What will he say to her for taking such liberties? All she can do is kneel and tell him her story. To her delight Jesus affirms her healing, and she can now begin to live again, to enjoy not just a healed body and situation, but go with his personal blessing of peace.

Good news for that woman, bad news for Jairus. While Jesus has been delayed by the woman, things have gone from bad to worse at his home. His daughter has died, and messengers have been sent to say, 'It's too late, don't bother Jesus now.' Jairus must have been devastated. If only there had been more time, if only . . . But Jesus tells him not to be afraid, but to believe, and taking Jairus, with Peter, James and John, goes on to the house. What meets them there is the mourning process already in operation, the crying, wailing and weeping; and when Jesus tells them to shut up, because the child is not dead only asleep, their weeping turns to laughter, the laughter of derision, no doubt some of it directed at Jairus for being so stupid as to trust Jesus in the first place.

Jesus takes the parents and his three close friends into the little girl's room, gently takes her hand and speaks to her. She opens her eyes and gets up – just like that! And – the lovely homely touch – Jesus turns and says, 'Give her something to eat!' After all, she is a normal, healthy twelve-year-old who needs her tea – it must have been quite some tea party!

So what had a frightened, sick woman and a desperate father in common? Surely it was faith to believe against the odds. To have the faith to just reach out a hand towards Jesus. To walk with him even through tears and jeers and look into the face of death itself with him. To believe that something would happen, whatever others said or thought. They were prepared to trust Jesus.

Yes, but back to those photographs in my newspaper, what hope for them? – and for all the others who suffer grief, pain, loss and despair?

I cannot and dare not offer some glib formula, or pretend I know the answer, or can produce a magic wand to banish suffering and death. What I do know is that Jesus has overcome suffering and death and he will give us all the strength and the courage we need. His promise is true, 'Because I live you will live also.' I see over and over again the reality of that in the lives of people who humanly speaking have no hope. The words of Jesus, 'Don't be afraid, only believe,' hold true for you and me today just as they did two thousand years ago. Trust him – for he is trustworthy.

Lord,
Suffering and death are real. I only have to pick
up the paper to know that. It is there, recorded
in stark words and pictures.
Suffering and death are real. I know it from my
own experience, and I am afraid.
In your love and power reach out to those who
suffer today, to those who mourn, those who
have lost hope.
Reach out to me too, Lord, and grant me your
peace.

A Question of Identity

(6.1–29)

When it was announced that George Carey was to
be the next Archbishop of Canterbury some people
were surprised, others even shocked. After all, he
was the son of a hospital porter, brought up on a
council estate in Dagenham. What sort of an archbishop would he be, especially as he had not been
to either Oxford or Cambridge? His background,
his family, even his teeth came in for criticism!
The fact that he had not only a degree but a docto-
rate was conveniently forgotten by some of his op-
ponents. Also, his 'track record' in the parochial
ministry, in theological colleges and as a bishop
seemed to count for nothing.

Dr Carey can count it a privilege, though, to follow in the great tradition, even of Jesus himself
who also found he was judged not by who he was or
the message he brought but by his background.
'Isn't he the carpenter, the son of Mary, and the
brother of James, Joseph, Judas and Simon? Aren't
his sisters living here?' (verse 3). Whoever heard of
a carpenter teaching and performing miracles? So he
was rejected in his home town. Jesus did not con-
form to the pattern they knew, they were blinded by
their tunnel vision and so failed to see who he was.
They denied themselves the opportunity, the God-
given opportunity, of receiving the gift of eternal
life, of healing and wholeness. Their lack of faith
restricted his ministry. The locals thought they
knew all there was to know about him, and they
were not prepared to see or to hear anything different. They were surprised that anyone like him
could do what he did, but still they could not accept

him. Jesus was amazed that, faced with the evidence of his power, the people still could not believe. It was stalemate, and it must have been heart-breaking for Jesus. His own friends, his own folk, and they didn't want to know.

We were talking about this in a house group one day in my parish, and all being rather self-righteous about it, saying how sad it was, and how stupid the people were not to recognise who Jesus really was. An elderly lady in the group smiled, and said, 'And what if he had come from Selby? I don't think we would have believed either.' Sheepishly we had to admit she was probably right!

A few days ago I heard two people opposite me on the train discussing someone who was very much in the news because of his expertise in a particular situation. One said to the other, 'I don't know what all the fuss is about, he's nobody. They used to live up by my auntie in Hull, his dad worked on the docks and he went to the same school as our Sid.' 'He's nobody . . .' I thought of the words of Jesus about a prophet respected everywhere but in his own home town! What was true for Jesus was also to be true for his followers. They too would find places where they were not accepted or recognised, and the only thing to do was to move on. Jesus sent his disciples out with his authority, not to be laden down with the luggage of worldly trappings but as ordinary travellers. If they were accepted, whether those who welcomed them were rich or poor, no matter, they must stay with them. They had good news for all who wanted to receive it, they were messengers of God's kingdom, and they were to keep moving so that as many as possible could have the opportunity to hear their message and receive it.

Someone else had heard about Jesus and come to a conclusion as to his identity – King Herod. Herod had had John the Baptist put to death because John had challenged him about his adulterous relationship, and the woman in question was determined to get rid of John in case Herod listened to him. Herodias used her guile in pandering to his pleasure in watching her daughter dance, and when Herod promised the girl anything she desired, her mother got her to ask for the head of John the Baptist. Herod was too proud a man to go back on his promise, and afraid to lose face, so John had to lose his head. John may have been put to death, but John's life and witness lived on in the memory of Herod, and so when he heard of Jesus, he was sure this was the same man come back to life, and he was frightened to death. He could not escape from condemnation, and he knew it.

When Jesus himself was put to death many, as Herodias had thought of John, thought they had got rid of him for ever, he would not trouble them any more. They were mistaken! Two thousand years on, the message of John is still heard, his challenge to turn from sin and death. The offer of freedom and life is still heard too. The invitation comes loud and clear, for Jesus lives and speaks and acts, yes today; and for those who hear and respond comes the joy of stepping out with him and for him.

It is said that 'truth will out' – we all stand under the judgement of the truth, and of the one who said, 'I am the way, the truth and the life'. If we choose to accept his truth then we will experience the glorious freedom he promised, and be free to serve. As the Victorian preacher F.W. Robertson said, 'Truth is given, not to be contemplated but to be done. Life is an action, not a thought.' Jesus asks not for our approval but for our obedience, not to discuss his authority but to submit to it, and in doing so to discover that his service is perfect freedom indeed.

Lord,
Thank you for reminding me that you speak
through all sorts of people, in many accents, in
every kind of situation. Open my ears to hear,
my eyes to see and my heart to accept with joy
your message and your messengers.

Food for Thought
(6.30–44)

If a survey was carried out to find the top ten Bible stories, I am pretty sure that the Feeding of the Five Thousand would come pretty high on the list. It is one of those very memorable accounts which stick in the mind and, for those who have ever been to Sunday school, an often repeated story. It is a gift to preachers on Missionary Gift Day, or Harvest Festival or stewardship weekends – how even a small and seemingly insignificant amount given to the Lord will be used beyond our imagining. If you read John's Gospel chapter 6, you will see that Jesus uses the incident to be the basis for his teaching on 'the bread of life', a reminder that there is more to life than having physical needs met; the spiritual side has to be nourished as well.

So often this account of the feeding of the five thousand is only thought about in the context of the hungry crowd and the miracle that took place. Have you ever thought of it in terms of the disciples, and the situation they found themselves in? Go back a few verses to verse 7 onwards. The disciples are being sent out on their first mission, exciting, demanding, and extremely exhausting. Then move on to verse 30 and try to imagine the scene, the disciples coming back to Jesus with all their news, their questions, so much to share with him. They were on a 'high', but it had taken so much out of them that they were on the point of collapse. Yet there was to be no let up in the demanding, punishing schedule – more and more people, more and more demands upon Jesus and the disciples – and Jesus recognises the vital need for some peace and quiet: 'Let us go off by ourselves to some place where we will be alone and you can rest for a while' – bliss!

Unfortunately, it didn't work out like that. While they were crossing over in the boat the people ran ahead and were there before them. The disciples must have been fed up to the teeth with people, but Jesus is so sorry for these needy people, he gives himself to them without stinting. Time goes on and time goes on and evening comes and the hunger pangs come on. So what? What would you have felt if you have been one of the disciples? What would your attitude have been? I have a good idea, for something similar happened to me a while back!

I had been through a very busy and tiring time, meeting deadlines, trying to cram far too much work into too short a time, with a number of extra demands being placed on me. A friend rang up, and noticing I seemed a little jagged at the edges said, 'You sound as though you could do with a day out. Come over tomorrow and we will have a quiet day, I'll get the sun-loungers out.' Just what I needed! I jumped at the chance. The day was warm and sunny and I set off early. My friend lives in a particularly beautiful spot, and I was looking forward to the pleasure of her company; she is fun to be with, and also has a wealth of wisdom. Just the person I needed to be with, to be able to unwind and relax.

The first hour was bliss, and then the phone rang. My friend came back into the garden looking serious. 'I'm sorry about this, but it's someone who is going through a bad time – family problems, a near nervous breakdown and now she has been told she has to have an operation. I've invited her over. You don't mind do you?' I mumbled, 'No, of course not,' but inside I minded very much indeed. I felt robbed of what I felt I was entitled to have, a day of peace, without people and their problems. Why hadn't my friend said she had a visitor, asked this woman to come tomorrow? Surely one day wouldn't have made so much difference?

Later that morning, a small, nervous-looking little woman arrived. She was hard work, and she kept looking at me sideways as though she expected me to bite her – maybe I looked as though I would! Over lunch she relaxed more, then I went and made some coffee and we all sat outside and enjoyed the garden. I noticed how my friend eased the conversation, in a very gentle but firm way guiding Joan – that was her name – into a more positive frame of mind. Then Joan looked at her watch. 'Good gracious, I must be getting back, but thank you both so much, you've been such a help. I really feel it's going to be all right now.' My friend said, 'Before you go, let's pray, and commit it to the Lord.' We sat and prayed quietly, then held hands and said the grace together. After Joan had gone my friend said, 'A pity about that, it's not been much of a day off for you, but I couldn't do any other could I?' I agreed, and anyway we still had a couple of hours left.

We went for a walk along the river, the water bubbling and tumbling beside us, the countryside looking at its summery best, the sky a brilliant blue, and the air sweet and warm. After tea I left for home and meandered along, enjoying the peace and quiet of the back lanes. It had been a good day, and actually meeting Joan, hearing her story, and seeing my friend supporting and encouraging her, had helped me too, given me some new insights into caring for folk with similar problems.

I think I understood a little how the disciples must have felt when they had been so busy serving others and sorting out other peoples' problems, and Jesus offered them a time of peace and quiet with him, only to have all those people turning up, demanding his attention. No wonder the disciples said, 'Send the people away, let them go . . .' Let them take their problems elsewhere, and leave us in peace. Instead, Jesus enlisted their help in preparing the crowd, and taking the little there was to hand, fed five thousand people, the disciples included, with plenty left over too. They were partners in a miracle which would be recorded for all time, a day to remember! I am pretty sure that, like me, the disciples felt rather resentful and frustrated when their peace was disturbed, their hopes for a quiet day dashed by that unwelcome intrusion. And yet, would they have changed it at the end of the day? I know my day was enhanced rather than hindered by seeing a cry for help responded to so graciously – and by being allowed to be in some small way a partner in that response.

Woody Allen once said, 'If you want to make God laugh, tell him your future plans!' He must laugh a lot as he looks at us so busy organising our lives to suit ourselves, sticking 'reserved for me' notices on tomorrow, next week, next year, next . . . If only we would remember that everything is 'DV' – *Deo volente* – by God's will, then we can say at the end of each day, *Deo gratias* – Thanks to God.

Lord,
Help me not to be resentful or selfish when my plans are thwarted by another's need, but to respond gladly as a partner in your loving purposes and find my joy in serving others, for your name's sake.

65

Beyond Belief

(6.45–56)

A free meal ticket for life! No wonder the crowd went wild with excitement. With Jesus as their leader they would never have to worry again. With him, the miracle man, they could overthrow their enemies, enjoy full health and full stomachs. What more did they want? Jesus knew what they were thinking, so he quickly sent the disciples away, arranging to meet them later, while he said goodbye to the crowd. Jesus needed time alone now with his Father, so he slipped quietly away from them all, to have space to be and to pray.

The disciples were making heavy weather rowing. They must have been very tired, and with the wind against them, they were just making no headway at all. From his vantage point Jesus could see they were in difficulties and went to them, walking on the water. Far from being comforted by the sight of Jesus they were petrified, thinking it was a ghost – for no one walks on water, it is an impossibility!

No one walks on water! Jesus did. Do you believe he did, or is it just an allegory? Were the disciples in such a state of exhaustion and shock that they imagined it, or did it really happen? I believe it did happen as Mark said. Jesus saw his friends were in need of him and he went to them – as simple as that. It was no more, no less a miracle than any of the other miracles which have been recorded. Jesus had to calm the disciples down, and he did it by his word of encouragement, and by getting into the boat with them so they could see it was really him. Even so, with him sitting there, and the sea calmed, they still could not take it in. Yet they had been part of the miracle as he fed the five thousand, they had seen it with their eyes, had even eaten the food themselves; but they were still confused. It was all too much for them, this walking on the water. They had set out to follow a great man, a wonderful teacher, a healer, but he was clearly more than that, things were happening that they could not explain. It was all beyond them, and they were afraid of the consequences.

Jesus can be a comfortable figure if we keep him within the pages of a book and within the walls of our church. It is when we realise that he is alive and ever present, now, that miracles are happening, things we cannot explain away, that we begin to get a little apprehensive. 'Too hot to handle' Jesus was when he was here on earth, and he is now!

There is only one explanation – he is God. Not a godly man, but as Paul puts it writing to the Colossians 'the Son has in himself the full nature of God' (Colossians 1.19).

Stuart Blanch, in *Encounters with Jesus* says this:

> This is a claim so staggering as to be beyond human comprehension for ever. In moments of insight we may draw nearer the truth, then like a moth before a flame, we are dissolved by it. This for me has been one of the uncomfortable aspects of ministry, to have to speak for and to represent a shining truth which is forever beyond my grasp, and mocks my attempts to articulate it for others. There are no easy answers. The Christ event remains an unfathomable, though luminous mystery.

So it is, and all we can do is marvel and wonder at God's love for us in Jesus, and realise that we are never alone, he is with us when we are struggling, seemingly on our own. When life threatens to overpower us, when our understanding and our strength seem of little avail, he comes, and if we will listen we too will hear his words: 'Courage, it is I, don't be afraid.' My mind may not be able to grasp it, but my heart can accept it.

The people who waited over on the other side for Jesus accepted him all right. You could say that they used him, and took advantage of him. They crowded in on him, pleading for help for themselves and others, and Jesus met their need, because he loved them, and wanted them to be well. He did not insist they understood, he just touched them at their point of need. Who are we to condemn them? Don't we try and use Jesus, to manipulate him, and take without giving so often? We have a long way to go, and a lot to learn, but hopefully, like the claim of British Rail, 'We are getting there!'

Almighty God,
your power is awesome, your holiness and your
greatness I cannot fathom, and your purposes
are beyond my imagination. Yet you chose to
reveal yourself in Jesus, so that I might begin to
realise something of your glory and your love.
Thank you!

Inside Out or Outside In?
(7.1–23)

For the Pharisees and the teachers of the law, Jesus posed a great problem. He did not have their seal of approval. He had not come up through their recognised channels. So they sought to discredit him. After all, if they who had followed so meticulously the religious tradition of centuries – and more – could show that Jesus failed to observe the laid-down, accepted practices, then he would be *'persona non grata'*; he would have no credibility, or standing. They made sure he was watched carefully, so that they could gather evidence against him. They soon found it, for Jesus and his disciples did not follow the rigid hand-washing code of practice, and so could be declared 'unclean', with the implication that his message was defiled as well, and could not be taken seriously by any law-abiding Jew.

So the well-washed accusers stated their case. But Jesus had the answer for them. He answered 'in kind', by reference to Scripture, but not the portion they wanted to hear! He went to the heart of the matter, the inside story rather than outward observances. He reminded his critics that they had overlaid the original law by their own man-made statutes, in order to suit their own covenience. He called them hypocrites for making so much of the outward show and paying so little attention to what really matters. The Oxford Dictionary describes a hypocrite as 'a pretender' and as coming from the Greek word *hypokrites* – someone acting a part. That word must have stung them, being called play-actors when they thought they were the genuine word of authority!

Jesus pressed home the point by reminding them of simple physical facts, that it is not what goes into a person, what he eats or drinks, that makes a person unclean, because it comes out in it the normal fashion. What does show a person up for what he is, is what comes from the heart – the lies, the evil ideas, the hate, the meanness. Those are the things which defile a person, and they cannot be washed away by water, or removed by some legal formula. A right relationship with God comes not from ceremonial practices, but through repentance, the cleansing of the spirit through forgiveness. It comes through a change of heart, being changed 'inside out' and not the other way round.

Jesus was certainly not thanked for making the point. In fact it only hardened the determination of the Pharisees and teachers to get rid of him. They could not tolerate what he showed them of their own deficiency of spiritual understanding and practice. They preferred to go on play-acting, rather than face up to reality.

It is easy for us to condemn them, to point the finger at their arrogance; but as the adage reminds us, 'When you point a finger at someone else you leave three pointing to yourself.' We are not immune from falling into the same trap. You and I may not be caught up in ritual hand-washing practices, or quibbles over the intricate small print on a tin of baked beans, but we all have the red herrings we choose to use when we are faced with moral or religious issues, especially when we may be in the wrong! We can prove very adept at turning things around to suit ourselves – we all do it at times. What about the pious expression we put on to cover up our temper? The 'in language' we use to divert attention from what we are really saying? And is the hand raised to heaven in the choruses, or extended to another during the Peace, a demonstration of love for God and neighbour, or a flag of convenience covering up our real intention? We may be able to fool others – although I don't believe we fool other people as often as we would like to think. We may even fool ourselves sometimes. But we cannot fool God. Jesus reminded the Pharisees of this when he said, 'You are the ones who make yourself look right in other people's sight, but God knows your hearts.' (Luke 16.15)

Our behaviour, our worship, our words, works and attitudes should arise out of a grateful heart, from the joyful recognition of God's mercy and grace towards us. We are called to be ourselves before God, not to put on a show to impress the gallery! We need to pray as the psalmist did,

Create a pure heart in me, O God,
    and put a new and loyal spirit in me.
Do not banish me from your presence;
    do not take your holy spirit away from me.
(Psalm 51.10,11)

Thank you Father, that you know me just as I am. You are not deceived by my play-acting. Help me now to recognise myself, to humbly acknowledge my need for change, and to accept with joy your transforming power in my life, through Jesus Christ. Amen.

A Vision for the Kingdom
(7.24–37)

Jesus did what he had told his disciples to do – if people wouldn't listen, and wouldn't accept the message, they should move on: 'Shake the dust off your feet.' Perhaps Jesus had had enough of the teachers of the law, with their petty picking over of points, or maybe he realised that trouble makers would hinder his ministry at that point. Whatever the reason, he went into Gentile territory on his own, 'away from it all' where he wasn't known, where he would have time to be alone. It was not to be!

A Gentile woman, having heard about him, came pleading for help for her daughter. The conversation that followed seems quite out of character for Jesus. His response to her plea for help seems very off-putting and rude. She had, of course, no claim on him, quite the opposite. She was a woman and a Gentile, and Jesus reminded her of that. He had come to his own people, the Jews, they were his priority. But the woman was not put off by his words. There must have been something in his tone of voice, or in his face, which gave her hope, and so she tossed back the remark, 'Even the dogs under the table eat the children's leftovers.' She knew she had no right to his help, but she knew that his love and power were limitless. For her, the crumbs of his comfort were sufficient.

What an encouragement it must have been to Jesus to hear her words, to see her faith. He had been given a very hard time by his own people, by those who professed to be men of faith and learning, and yet here was this foreign woman who had more insight than any of them. Her answer was the key not just to her daughter's healing, but perhaps to the opening up of Jesus' mission to the whole world. He saw here the response he longed to see from his own people, and the question he must have pondered on was answered. When, before his ascension, he commissioned his friends to 'Go throughout the whole world and preach the gospel to all mankind' (Mark 16.15), had not his experience of that day been a pointer towards his world view? The woman took his word for it that her daughter would be healed, and her faith was rewarded by the sight of her daughter made whole. Persistence had paid off; something we should all bear in mind!

As Jesus returned home another person was brought to him for help, a man unable to ask for help for himself, for he was deaf and dumb. Jesus took him away from the crowd, for the poor man must have been petrified by all that was going on, and not being able either to understand or to make himself understood. Jesus used visual means to show the man that he would be healed. The touch, the look, those were the means of communication the man understood. Jesus restored that man's total means of communication; he was able to hear and to speak. The crowd went wild with excitement. Here was the living proof of the power of Jesus. It was no use Jesus urging them to keep quiet about what had happened, they just couldn't keep the good news to themselves.

But Jesus did not want to be seen merely as a miracle worker and a healer. The danger was that people would flock to him because of that. He had so much more to give, the offer of new life in the kingdom of God. But most people would rather settle for a full stomach or the relief of pain and infirmity in this life than think about the future. It seemed to have no relevance for them.

In the Sermon on the Mount, Jesus emphasised the need to have a hunger and thirst for the spiritual aspect of life, a vision to see beyond material satisfaction to the kingdom of God. 'So do not start worrying: "Where will my food come from? or my drink? or my clothes?" (These are the things the pagans are always concerned about.) Your Father in heaven knows that you need all these things. Instead, be concerned above everything else with the kingdom of God, and with what he requires of you, and he will provide you with all these other things' (Matthew 6.31–33).

Are we any different from the people who flocked to Jesus for help then? 'Heal me . . . help me . . . give me . . .' So much of our praying is just this, a shopping list marked 'for me'. Of course we need 'these other things,' as Jesus called them. We all want to be fed, to be well, to be happy – but first things first. Knowing God, seeking to do his will, sharing the vision of his kingdom with others, these are the things that matter ultimately, that satisfy in the end, and give lasting joy. Our world is suffering from a chronic disease called 'me first', and because of this it stands on the brink of disaster. It is not enough to condemn that attitude in others. It is for us to break free, by the grace of God, and turn our sights, our hopes and our efforts on his kingdom on earth and in heaven. An earth-shattering concept, lived out and worked out in the light of all eternity!

Father,
It is so easy to pray the words, 'Your kingdom come, your will be done on earth as it is in heaven.' I find it so hard to put my prayer into practice. Give me a vision of your kingdom, turn my dreams into desire, and my desire into determination that I may not be satisfied with anything less than doing your will as a servant of the King.

Bread and More Bread
(8.1–21)

You may be tempted to think you have read this before, the account of the feeding of the multitude by Jesus with a few loaves and fishes. Go back a couple of chapters in Mark's Gospel, and there it is, the feeding of the five thousand. And now here it is again, but this time it is four thousand. Was it that someone just could not add up? They might be forgiven for that – after all, a crowd takes some counting, and what is a thousand here or there? But look more closely: there are very definite and important differences. For a start, they occurred in two different places. The first miracle of the feeding of the five thousand took place in Galilee, to mainly Jewish people. Here the four thousand were in Gentile territory, near Decapolis, so the people would be for the most part Gentiles – they were very particular about keeping to their own areas; there was no love lost between them. The five thousand people were hungry all right, having had nothing to eat all day, but the four thousand were desperate; they had gone without food for three days, and so were in danger of collapse, of being unable through weakness of body to attempt the journey home.

The people, the areas, the situations may have been entirely different, but one thing was the same, the compassion of Jesus as he looked at people in need. He knew what it was like to be hungry, to be out all day without food. He knew what it was like to be desperately in need – remember the wilderness experience? He knew and he responded, taking those pathetically small human resources of bread and fish and providing a meal to satisfy and sustain the whole crowd. Only when he had fed them – spiritually and physically – did he send them away. They had come to hear a preacher, they were fed by the word of God – food for hungry souls – but they also had bodies that needed sustaining. Jesus knew the importance of 'daily bread' and powerfully attended to that need also. He saw people as people – they were not 'souls on legs' but individuals who needed help.

I wonder whether we learn from Jesus' example or if we lean too heavily to one side or the other? There are those who sneer at 'the social gospel', at those who concern themselves with attending to immediate need such as poverty, homelessness, hunger and deprivation. There are again, others who see the preaching of the gospel, evangelism, outreach, missionary work – whatever you choose to call it – as secondary. I use the word 'gospel' deliberately, for what is the gospel but good news from God – and that surely is about every aspect of life. Thankfully there now seems to be a growing fusion between the two viewpoints, and a desire to meet human need in whatever form, wherever it is seen.

But back now to our passage. For Jesus, there was to be no respite. There were people who were very anxious to destroy him, to debase his teaching and belittle his actions. The Pharisees who came to argue with him asked for a sign of his power. Not content with what they knew had happened, they demanded a spectacular show of power, not because they wanted to believe but because they were determined not to. No wonder Jesus groaned – the tragedy of it all! Here were people who were well versed in God's word, intelligent, trained, so sure of their position before God, and yet delighting to put up obstacles to faith over and over again. Not even a sign from heaven would convince them; and there was no need. They had all the signs they needed, and they were blind to them. They had turned their back on the one who could have given them all they needed. In the end, all Jesus could do was turn his back on them, and go on his way with others.

The others here were his disciples, privileged indeed. They had not only seen the miraculous feeding of the crowds, but had been part of it. They had distributed the food to the crowd; they knew it was real all right, hadn't their hands held the bread and fish, and gathered up the remains? Hadn't their eyes seen, their ears heard, their bodies received, that same food? Yet what were they bothered about as they rowed back with Jesus across the lake – the fact they were short of bread! They had completely forgotten the implications of what they had been part of; its significance had been lost on them. Jesus patiently tried to remind them of what had happened, went step by step through it, but it was no use; they failed to connect, they could only focus on the immediate.

Jesus groaned over the Pharisees; he must have groaned over his friends as well. They did not mean to be difficult, they just were! As Jesus looked at his friends, could he have regretted choosing them? They were more of an encumbrance than a help. Knowing he had but a short time left with them, how would they manage, how could they cope? They would need a friend, a powerful friend – someone like Jesus, who would be always with them to help them, to enable them, to strengthen them. The Pharisees had demanded a sign from heaven. It would not be given to them; but this little group of friends, they would receive a sign all right – a most dramatic sign that would change them, because it would be no outward manifestation that would disappear after the initial excitement, but would take root within them, be with them for ever; and not just with them, but with all who would believe. But that was in the future. Dark days lay ahead. The friends would have to cope with more than the worry over a loaf of bread, they would be tested and tried beyond their imagination. But it would be all right – in the end.

Lord,
I so soon get thrown by circumstances.
I panic over little things,
faith goes out the window.
Be patient with me.
Remind me of all the way you have brought me,
provided for me.
Feed me with your living word
that I may grow in understanding,
in trust and love.
Don't give up on me, will you?
– But I know you won't,
because you promised you wouldn't,
and you always keep your promises.

What do You Say?
(8.22–38)

Jesus performed many healing miracles which were immediate and complete – no half measures. Yet this blind man seemed to be healed in two stages. He got his sight all right, but it was out of focus – 'I can see people but they look like trees walking about' – and it was not until Jesus laid hands on him the second time that he saw clearly. Strange! Was it the atmosphere of the place, the man's condition, or intentional? Jesus so often used miracles as a pointer to spiritual truths; for instance the feeding of the five and four thousands pointed to 'the bread of life'. Could it have been to show his disciples that 'seeing' – insight – is often a gradual thing? I can think back to events in my own life when, had I understood completely at the time, it would have been too much for me. In some situations it was better, kinder and in the end more valuable, to have had a gradual awakening to the true facts of the matter. When Jesus was speaking to his disciples just before his death he said, 'I have much more to tell you, but now it would be too much for you to bear . . .' (John 16.12).

Was the miracle of the healing of the blind man at Bethsaida such an example? Whatever the reason, it was after it that Jesus began to question his disciples as to his identity – 'Tell me, who do people say I am?' The gentle approach, almost casual. They would be eager to tell him about other people's views, reporting back what they had heard, falling over themselves to share it. But then came the direct question, 'What about you? Who do you say I am?' I am sure you could have cut the air with a knife, as they stood still in their tracks, hardly daring to breath, to think, to look. It was Peter, that impetuous, lovable hot-headed and hot-hearted man, who blurted straight out with it: 'You are the Messiah.' The truth with all its stark, awesome, frightening meaning. There was no going back now. Maybe the words of declaration also brought a sense of relief. They all knew now where they stood – or thought they did.

Now Jesus revealed to them what that would involve. He painted the picture in vivid colours, of the path of 'the Son of Man' – the Messiah, the one who would suffer, be rejected, be put to death, but would rise again after three days. Peter must have been dumbfounded, shocked. After all, he knew who Jesus was now. Nothing was impossible, victory was assured. So why did Jesus go on about failure – for so it must have seemed to him. Peter was never one to hold back his feelings, or slow to put voice to thoughts, and as Jesus' 'number one' he made it his business to speak plainly: there must be none of this defeatism, that was no way for the Messiah to behave.

The response was immediate and frightening. 'Get away from me, Satan.' To speak like that to Peter, his friend, the one who understood, the one who was right behind him, the one who would do anything, go anywhere! Peter, the one who thought he saw so clearly – and now it seemed he couldn't see the wood for the trees. Had he forgotten all Jesus had tried to say? As Jesus must have been delighted when Peter made his profession of faith, he was also alive to the dangers of such knowledge. The devil uses many and varied methods to tempt and distract people, and here Jesus recognised again the subtlety that Satan used in the wilderness, spoken through the lips of his friend. The agonised

cry: 'Get away from me, Satan', was not just directed at Peter but at the one who was trying to get
at him through Peter. Jesus had to meet this head
on, and so he gathered both his disciples and the
crowd, and spelled out what it meant to be on his
side, what it would demand of them. They must
make the choice, decide what and who mattered
most, and take the consequences. It was a matter of
life or death, there were no half-way options.

John Young, in his book *Jesus the Verdict*, says:

Being a Christian always involves a sort of death.
It means holding Jesus' standards in a world
which does not much like those standards. Trying to care about people when it would be much
easier not to bother. Trying to change our own
wrong attitudes and habits . . . but paradoxically,
Jesus insists that the cross is about life, not only
about death . . .

When Jesus spoke about carrying a cross, those
who heard him were in no doubt what that meant,
they would have seen that sight all too often, and
shuddered at the thought of it ever happening to
them. It was 'a fate worse than death', a nightmare.
Yet Jesus forced them to think about it, the stark
reality of what it meant to be on his side.

Jesus still issues the challenge to those today
who might think of being a Christian as an easy
option, a joy ride, a way of commanding respect. He
forces us personally to face up to what it really
means to belong to him. We may try to wriggle out
of the implications, we may say 'But times have
changed', or 'It won't be like that for me.' His voice
will again thunder in rebuke, to us this time: 'Get
away from me, Satan' – and we will either slink
away because we cannot take his challenge or turn

to him, towards the cross, submit to our own death for his sake, and so to life. The challenge has not changed, nor the cost, nor the final outcome. The choice is ours.

Lord Jesus,
You are the King of glory,
You are the prince of peace.
You are Lord over life and death,
yours is the victory.
It is easy to say that, Lord,
so easy to sing about it,
but the truth frightens me,
the cost appals me.
Suffering and death –
I want to avoid them at all costs.
'At all costs' –
but then that's what it is, isn't it?
All, everything,
the price of victory,
the price you paid for my life.
Surely there must be an easier way,
quicker, cleaner,
but if there is
you don't give it as an option.
There is only one way, your way.
Lord, give me strength to walk in it,
today and always.

On Top of the World
(9.1–29)

It had been a depressing meeting. Our group had worked hard and long for a particular cause. We were committed to it, others had seemed to support it, but the promised and hoped-for support had not materialised. We had to admit we were beaten, for the time being anyway. Someone muttered, rather half-heartedly, 'Well, as it says, "when one door shuts another door opens." ' At that our chairman said, with great feeling, 'I think you've got the quotation wrong, it's "when one door shuts another gets slammed in your face." ' It certainly felt like that for us that night.

The three closest friends of Jesus might have agreed with that sentiment as they toiled up the mountain behind Jesus. So many things seemed not to make sense. There was the continued opposition of the religious leaders to Jesus, always trying to pick arguments with him, to belittle his work. The crowds were rather tiresome, wanting Jesus for what they could get out of him and demanding more and more. And Jesus kept going on about suffering and death, and that they had to face up to that too if they wanted to follow him. It really was rather wearying and worrying. What had they let themselves in for? Where would it all end?

They were so tired, they were more than ready for a rest as they arrived at the top. In fact in Luke's Gospel account we are told that 'Peter and his companions were sound asleep' (Luke 9.32), when something happened to Jesus. One minute he had been the familiar friend and leader, dressed in his ordinary clothes, as they were; the next, as they looked up at him, he was in dazzling white. Not just ordinary white, but shining, glowing, out-of-this world white. He was not alone, either. On one side was Elijah, the greatest of all the prophets who had been. On the other side stood Moses, the law-giver, the one who had been given the law by God himself. Here were the two greatest figures in history and they were talking with Jesus, acknowledging him. It was beyond understanding. All the three disciples could do was gaze on this glorious, awesome, holy scene. This was it! They could forget all that talk about suffering and death, forget the disappointments, the arguments, forget the tiredness, if only it could be like this forever – and why not? Why not remain there, sharing the glory, the power, the joy?

Peter speaks – as usual he rushes in, feeling he knows what is wanted – he wants to press the pause button on life right *now*. 'Teacher, how good it is we are here! We will make three tents, one for you, one for Moses, one for Elijah.' In other words, 'Let's take up residence here, forget the rest of the world,' the world that lay down the mountain. It was the first thing that came into his head. He was overcome by what was happening, as the others were, but he knew this was glorious, and he wanted to keep it that way. Even as he spoke it was over: the cloud rolled over the scene, but from beyond it came a voice: 'This is my own dear Son – listen to him.' And then there was Jesus, as he was before, and alone.

It was over, whatever it was. But they knew it had really happened. It was real enough. What a story they had to tell now! Now Jesus forbade them to speak of it, until after he had risen from the dead. So they were back, it seemed, to square one, suffering and death. Jesus explained to them that the forerunner had already come, in John the Baptist, and look what had happened to him. He was the one they had looked for, and yet rejected. It would be just the same for Jesus himself. There was no easy short cut to victory.

They did as they were told, and until after Jesus had risen from the dead they kept their silence about what had happened on that mountain, the scene they had shared. They kept silence, but within themselves they must have gone over it time after time after time, knowing that, although they did not comprehend the significance, it had given them a glimmer of hope beyond their understanding, a treasured sign of hope for all time.

Life today can be very tedious, tiring and frightening. It can seem at times 'one step forwards and two steps backwards'. That meeting I was at was not the first time I had felt, 'Is it all worth it?' and no doubt it was not the last, but I know in my own experience the glorious power of Jesus, the risen, ascended, glorified Lord. There have been moments when I have known this so powerfully, and they have all been totally unexpected. I have had my own 'mountaintop' experiences. Sometimes they have literally been, if not on a mountain-top, on hill-tops. One particularly vivid memory is of when I stood on the North Yorkshire Moors looking across to the sea near Whitby. Another time was in a remote country church, hidden away in a green and golden valley in autumn. Sometimes they have been in the ordinary everyday events of life, moments of sheer exhilaration, of knowing the immediate presence of the Lord.

I am reminded of St John, in exile, and of his visions of heaven and the hereafter. He could write, 'After this I looked, and lo, in heaven, an open door . . .' (Revelation 4.1 RSV). I believe we are granted these experiences to encourage and assure us on our journey of faith. Just as Jacob, when feeling so far from home and God, experienced his vision of a stairway reaching from earth to heaven and angels ascending and descending, could then say, 'The Lord is here! He is in this place, and I didn't know it!' (Genesis 28.16). My feelings are often the same as Peter's on the mount of Transfiguration: 'It is good to be here' – 'Oh that it could remain like this for ever' – but it is not to be. We are given these glimpses of glory as an encouragement to go on travelling, a renewing experience on the way to the final glory. In the meanwhile, there is work to be done, a world to live in, people to care for, good news to share.

As Jesus and his three friends came down the mountain, they were met by arguing officials, a demanding crowd, a frightened father with a demented son, and disciples unable to cope with either the questions or conditions. Jesus, by his presence, brought order out of the chaos, release, health and hope. To the question, 'Why couldn't we drive the spirit out?' Jesus answered his disciples, 'Only prayer can drive this kind out, nothing else can.'

That is something we need to remember and practise when we feel the world is too much, when we feel inadequate, and that the situation is hopeless. It is the only answer. It is the answer that Jesus gave and still gives us. To pray on in faith and obedience, to go on going on, sustained by those glimpses of glory which the Lord in his love gives us – if we will keep our eyes on him!

Lord,
Thank you for the glimpses of your glory that we experience, those 'mountain-top' experiences which are indeed a foretaste of heaven.
Thank you for the power of prayer, the opportunity we have at all times to come into your presence to receive your strength, so that we may work and witness to your praise and glory.

Remember the Child
(9.30–42)

The message was just not getting through to them. Was it that they did not understand, could not understand or would not understand? Before we condemn the disciples, let us look into our own lives. How many times when we hear an unpalatable message do we turn off, or decide it is for others, not for us personally? The disciples did not want to hear about suffering and death. They were far too interested in their own standing, each jockeying for top positions. Their conversation became rather heated until Jesus asked them what their argument was about. His gentle but firm insistence that they speak out only served to reduce them to silence, a very uneasy silence at that.

Jesus was perfectly aware of the topic of conversation; the disciples were condemned by their own reluctance to answer. So Jesus did what he often did, and gave them a visual aid, this time standing a small child in front of them. The child was quite unafraid, for Jesus had his arms around him; he was safe and secure within those strong, loving arms; he did not ask for anything, he had all he needed. Jesus used that situation to teach his disciples the lesson they so badly needed to learn, that greatness is not position or power but openness, trust and obedience. Here was a child with no rights, no power, no strength, but in God's eyes as important as the wisest, richest and most powerful person on earth – and in fact more so, for a child needs even more protection, encouragement and love than an adult, who can do a certain amount for himself.

Children were very special people to Jesus, to his Father and so they must be to his followers. Some of the sternest words ever issued by Jesus concerned the treatment of children: 'If anyone should cause one of these little ones to lose his faith in me, it would be better for that person to have a large millstone tied around his neck and be thrown into the sea.' Jesus did not say that lightly, but as a strong warning to anyone who would disregard the needs of a child or take advantage of his helplessness.

In the last few years cases of child abuse have seemed to be growing in number, whether because of a greater awareness or that they occur more often; but it is evil and tragic, and a very sad reflection on life today. The words of Jesus are as clear and firm today as when he spoke them while here on earth two thousand years ago. Children are a precious gift to be cared for, to be honoured and protected. They have a God-given right to enjoy their innocence and must be allowed and encouraged to discover and grow in freedom, a freedom that also protects and shelters them from anything or anyone that would hurt, maim or pervert them.

Thank God for those who have taken seriously to heart the command of Jesus to care for little ones. Thank God for their faithfulness and love. Do we, though, see the care of children as a priority in our church or community? Do we do anything for them personally? I know how difficult it is to get people to teach in Sunday school, run youth clubs, even give a hand in the crèche. I hear the grumbles of good Christian people when a child cries during a service, or when a couple of toddlers decide to go and play games in the aisle. I know my own feelings when the noise level goes above what I consider acceptable. I get edgy and selfishly wish the parents would take them out. I am not too keen on sticky fingers and sicky faces! Yet my greatest joys have been when those same little folk have been brought up for a blessing, or come jumping with pleasure towards me to be held, to be touched, when they so trustingly run up to me, for they have completely forgotten I had glared or tut-tutted at them; and I am thankful to them for giving me another chance. These are the real VIPs, and their confidences and smiles worth more than any gilt-edged invitation cards. They have so much to teach me about love and acceptance, about forgiveness and the joy of living each moment to the full. I just pray I may not get too old to learn!

Lord,
As you set that little child in front of your disciples for an example, may I too learn the lesson of simple trust and obedience, and follow your example and command to care and protect the young and the vulnerable from hurt or harm.

Cut it Out!

(9.43–50)

Is there such a place as hell? If so, what is it like? I believe that there is such a place, not because I find it easy or pleasant to believe in, but because Jesus spoke very directly and seriously about hell, and gave constant warnings about it. He did not set out to frighten us, to give us nightmares, or to use it as moral blackmail to induce us to be good, but to warn us because he loves us. As any parent, teacher or adult friend will graphically paint the dangers of going into certain situations, like playing with matches, going off with strangers, meddling with electrical devices or living a loose sexual life, Jesus spells out the dangers of disregarding God's laws, the consequences of disobedience. We are not sent to hell, we go by our own choice, for free will, the power to choose, is God's gift to us – otherwise we would be less than humans, mere robots or puppets. At the end of the day we make our own decision between heaven and hell. The gate of heaven is wide open to us, as we affirm in the *Te Deum* '. . . you (Jesus) overcame the sting of death, and opened the kingdom of heaven to all believers.' No one forces us through the gates of heaven or hell, we choose our direction and our destination.

So by my reading and understanding of Scripture I am warned of the possibility of hell as well as encouraged and promised the reality of heaven. Hell does exist, I am in no doubt of that – but what is it like? Is it at all like the traditional pictures, almost straight out of horror films, of grinning devils shovelling people away into the flames? I can think of some horrendous paintings I have seen of the torment of hell, in beautiful old churches as well as in art galleries of both classical and modern art. I think of the York Mystery Plays, of sitting in the beautiful Museum Gardens and seeing hell open up before my eyes, fire and smoke, sulphur fumes and all, a dramatic presentation of 'hell and damnation'. Jesus, speaking to his disciples in this passage, likens hell to the Jerusalem rubbish tip called Gehenna, 'the valley of Hinnom', the site feared and despised because it was indeed 'the pits'.

Some modern theologians would hold that hell is not a physical place but a state of mind, of separation from God. The Archbishop of York, Dr John Habgood wrote in the York Diocesan Newspaper in June 1991:

> Hell is a subjective reality. We can create it for ourselves and in ourselves. It is the real possibility of contracting into total self-absorption, and its sense of everlastingness is a testimony to the indestructible nature of human personality. The ultimate abuse of our human freedom is the unwillingness to open ourselves to love, not even to infinite love. The torments we experience in such a subjective hell are the torments we inflict upon ourselves, and the closed gates of that hell are the gates of despair, a despair which sees no possibility of escape unless grace can somehow break through.

Whatever view you take of hell it is surely to be a place to be avoided at all costs. It is a terrible prospect, the prospect of eternal separation from God, who is the source of love and light and goodness. The words of Jesus challenge us as to our use of our hands, our feet, our eyes. What are we holding on to, walking into, looking at? Beauty or ugliness, loving or hating, God's grace or the lure of the devil?

It is so easy to think that we are above all this, that we can 'do our own thing', tamper with evil, fool around with things we know to be wrong, and be untouched by it all. Jesus say, 'Cut it out!' – stop while you have a chance, before the gates of hell clang shut behind you, and you are locked in to a situation that you cannot get out of.

It can be very hard to cut ourselves off from a situation, maybe a relationship we know is wrong, even a hobby or a job, a particular stance; but surely it is better to be deprived of that pleasure than to wind up in hell? Jesus talks about being purified by fire, about being preserved by salt. Fire burns, salt stings, but sometimes we have to choose the way that hurts for the ultimate blessing. When we know that surrender to the will of God, when we are willing to be purified, to be cleansed by him, then we can live in peace and harmony, not just in this life but for all eternity, in heaven with God forever.

Lord,
I know you love me so much you would never
send me to hell, but I know too that I could by
my own will send myself there. Keep me close to
you, alert to your voice, obedient to your word,
and walking in your ways of peace and light,
that I may know the joy of all eternity which is
your gift, your free offer of grace, both now and
for evermore.

Made in Heaven?
(10.1–12)

A few months ago I had the pleasure and privilege
of conducting the wedding of our daughter Alison's
best friend Lisa, to Mark. The wedding photograph,
a special reminder of that very happy day, stands
with others in our lounge. Another is of our own
wedding day, June 1960, so a much younger Peter
and Margaret Cundiff! The other picture which
takes pride of place is of my parents celebrating
their diamond wedding, sixty years of togetherness!
Sixty years span those three photographs, and we
count ourselves fortunate that in these days we can
look back on such happy memories, for the divorce
rate today is alarming. More than one in three marriages breaks down, and the length of time marriages last gets ever shorter, with at the other end of
the scale, marriages which seemed stable over
many years also failing in greater numbers. The
question of the remarriage of divorced persons in
church still rumbles on in the Church of England.
While some denominations do allow this, the
Roman Catholic Church takes the firmest stand of
all against it.

Yet the thorny question of divorce is no new
thing; in fact in the time of Moses it was allowed,
as Jesus reminded the Pharisees who tried to trap
him with the question, 'Does our law allow a man
to divorce his wife?' A man could divorce his wife
for the most trivial reason, such as burning his dinner or talking too much – he simply had to give her
a letter, a bill of divorcement as it was called, and
she was sent out of the house, with no come back,
no means of support. Women were seen as objects,

with no legal rights of their own, completely at the will and whim of their husbands. He could easily get rid of her, but it was very difficult indeed for a woman to be able to divorce him. With divorce so easy for the man, a woman had no real security. The threat always hung over her; she could be put out on her ears for the slightest thing. Jesus tried to show them that marriage as God intended is a loving, lasting relationship, a oneness of flesh, of life, of commitment. This should be the norm, not the exception. God joins the two together as part of his loving purpose for them to be one – for life; held together in harmony and security, not in a rigid legal prison, as some would see it.

While times may have changed, the pain of divorce, of broken relationships, and the problems they cause still remain the same. People get hurt, lives are ruined – not just the two parties but the whole family situation, and especially where there are children involved. Sadly, so often the partners jump into another marriage 'on the rebound', which may also come unstuck because the first situation was never really resolved; and the cycle of unhappiness, failure and despair runs on. This is not a 'hard-liner' approach, but a simple statement of fact. When my parents married, back in the difficult days of the early Thirties, they had to contend with many problems, but they stuck together because they loved one another and they intended to live out their marriage vows, regardless of what happened. As is often said, 'Marriages may be made in heaven but they have to be worked out here on earth.'

The marriage service reminds those coming to marriage that it is 'for better for worse, for richer for poorer, in sickness and in health . . .' Marriage is an act of faith, in God, in each other, for the future.

Sadly, some flounder, for all sorts of reasons, but sometimes it seems that a couple do not give the marriage a fair chance of survival, for they start off by seeing the avenue of divorce open if things do not work out as they planned. Divorce becomes easier; already we have what are called 'quicky divorces'. It is tragic, so far from the ideal God gave of the joy he intended to come from marriage. Society needs to be built upon the stability of family life, rooted in the home. When marriages tear apart so does the very structure of society. I thank God for the work of the Mothers' Union, dedicated to upholding the sanctity of marriage, to strengthening and encouraging Christian marriage and family life, and at the same time holding and supporting those who are finding it difficult, those whose marriages fall by the wayside. The Mothers' Union does that on an international, national and local scale. But it is also something we should all strive to do, man or woman, married or single, pointing always towards the ideal, but with compassion and understanding, care and concern for those who fail, so following in the spirit of Christ.

Father,
Thank you for the gift of human love, for its expression in marriage and family life, for all the joy experienced in loving and sharing together. Please help those who are finding their marriage difficult, those who have been betrayed, neglected or rejected, where love has died or has been destroyed. Help us not to judge but to care, and to support them with the spirit of compassion and understanding, for Christ's sake.

A Sense of Value

(10.13–31)

There are some things you are never allowed to
forget. A story is recounted over and over again,
just to make you feel embarrassed, or so it seems.
In our family we all have quite a selection which
we refer to when we feel one member is getting a
little too sure of himself or herself. One such is told
against me, but I will share it with you!

A few years ago, when our daughter Alison was
in her early teens, I had to go to a meeting at
Bishopthorpe Palace, the home of the Archbishop
of York. Some very important people would be
there, including of course the Archbishop, and it
was to conclude with tea. Alison and her friend
wanted to come for the ride to York, so I took them
but with stern instructions that they were not to
come into the Palace, but to wait in the car for me,
parked well down the drive. So having given them
the spare car key, some pocket money and sweets, I
went off to my meeting.

Imagine my horror when, in the middle of tea,
through the front door of the Palace came the two
girls, without a care in the world. 'Hullo mum.' I
tried to look as though I had never seen them before
in my life, but at the same time making it clear they
were to go away, and do as they had been told. Too
late, they were being offered tea and chocolate cake,
and accepting it. I thought of the Palace carpet, a
very pale shade, and of the crumbs. The girls were
very happy, very chatty too, making themselves
very much at home. I was feeling anything but!

Later, as we drove home, I grumbled at them,
reminding them of my instructions. 'But mum, it

wasn't our fault,' said Alison. 'This man came and asked us what we were doing, and we said we were waiting for you, and he said where were you, and we told him, and he said go in, and they asked us if we would like a piece of cake and . . . and you were ashamed of us!' I had to admit it, I had been. Well, it wasn't quite the done thing to gatecrash a tea at Bishopthorpe Palace was it? But they had been invited in, they were quite normal girls, and did say please and thankyou, and in fact got on very well with the other rather older and more sedate guests. The then Archbishop, Stuart Blanch, told me later how nice it had been to meet the girls, so there had been no need for me to get so hot under the collar. I remember I did have the good grace to admit I had been wrong, when Alison said, 'You thought we would let you down, and we didn't did we?'

The account of the annoyance felt by the disciples when people brought their children wanting Jesus to bless them always reminds me of how I felt that day at Bishopthorpe Palace. I know the feeling! The disciples knew how busy Jesus was, how limited his time, the demands and pressures upon him, and they concluded he must be saved for the more important people, not pestered by mums and their children. After all, what use were they, and anyway, the children did not understand what was going on, they were too young. No, send them away, Jesus had better things to do.

In fact the incident made Jesus very angry, not with the mothers or their children, but with his disciples. They were the ones who lacked understanding, who failed to realise Jesus' sense of priorities. Jesus had time for children, and the account tells us that 'he took the children in his arms, placed his hand on *each one* of them and blessed them . . .' The care and love he showed

them, placing his hands 'on each one', made it clear
that he had all the time in the world for them; and
again, as in the incident related in Chapter 9, he
used that incident to try to bring home the lesson
to be learned through a child.

Anyone who wanted to come to Jesus was welcomed, they were never turned away. The man
who came running to him was welcomed warmly –
and I have the feeling that the disciples gave him
the 'red carpet treatment'. After all, he was just the
sort of person Jesus needed to have on his side, rich,
good and keen – what more do you ask for? Just the
sort of person who would receive a very warm
wlecome into any home, organisation, or church. A
useful sort of person, a real asset. But Jesus did ask
for more, and he asked for the one thing the man
was not prepared to give, himself. Sure enough he
wanted to have eternal life, he wanted to know the
secret of living life as it should be; but he also
wanted to hold on to what he had, in his case his
money and possessions. It was a struggle, but in the
end he turned and went away, very sad to do so, but
the price was too high. In Matthew's Gospel we are
told he was a young man, in Luke that he was a
Jewish leader, so he had evidently got everything
going for him; but what he had, got in the way of
what he needed most. The disciples must have
stood by open-mouthed as the man walked away.
Couldn't Jesus have toned down the challenge a bit,
eased him in? What a loss!

Peter was quick to comment, though. His mind
had worked out the situation and so, since he and
the others had given up everything for Jesus, had
done what was asked of them, well, what was in it
for them? The thought of getting a hundredfold return suited them very well – but there was a sting
in the tail as Jesus added '. . , and persecutions as

well . . .' No, that cast a damper on it. Maybe, as Jesus said that, there was a sense of unease amongst the disciples, a feeling that things might not be going as they hoped. Perhaps, as they looked at the receding figure of the young man on his way home, some of them may have wondered whether he had in the end made the more sensible decision.

I quite often meet very enthusiastic people who want to know how to lead 'the good life', what they must do to enjoy peace of mind and heart, to serve God, to advance his kingdom. Their enthusiasm flags a bit as they begin to realise it will touch their pocket, their time, their talents. It may mean a change in their present lifestyle, their ambition, their freedom. I have seen many walk away, just as sad as that man did from the presence of Jesus. I cannot be less than honest with them, for Jesus never was. 'You are always going on about total commitment, it frightens people off, you know,' I was told rather accusingly one day. But then, that is what the Christian life is about, total commitment, one hunded per cent. It does not require everybody to sell up, give up their home, or their job. For some it may, but what Jesus did was to put his finger on the thing that was most important to that man. It has been said, 'If Jesus is not Lord of all, he is not Lord at all' – it is true. Eternal life is a free gift, but it will cost you everything; that is the paradox of the challenge of Jesus Christ to each individual.

Jesus said we must receive the kingdom of God like a child. Think back to the children who came to him. No strings attached, all they wanted was to be with Jesus, nothing else mattered. Sadly, as we grow up, other considerations creep in, we 'want to have our cake and eat it', but it is not possible. We need to learn the lesson shown by the joyful self-abandonment of children, so that we may feel the touch of Jesus on our lives. The alternative is that we settle for the transient rather than the eternal treasures of life. It all depends on which we place the greater value, doesn't it?

Set me free, Lord, from what I have, so I may receive all you want to give me.
May I sit light to the possessions of this life, that I may know the joy of being possessed by your love for all eternity.

What do You Want?
(10.32–52)

Not for nothing were James and John nicknamed 'men of thunder' by Jesus (see Mark 3.17). They had a fiery, impatient temperament, but coupled with a steadfast devotion to Jesus and his cause. In Luke's Gospel we are told of the time when they suggested to him they should call down fire from heaven to destroy the people of one unsympathetic village! (Luke 9.52–5). Jesus was king, they were sure of that; his kingdom was supreme, of that they needed no convincing. It was just that they saw king and kingdom in their own terms, based on their experience of the world as they saw it. They also had a wonderful picture in their minds of the splendid scene when Jesus would come into his kingdom, and who might be flanking him either side as his 'top people'! But they wanted to make sure of it. Quite convinced their request was well founded, they approached their Master: 'Teacher there is something we want you to do for us.' When Jesus asked them what it was they told him plainly, 'When you sit on your throne in your glorious kingdom, we want you to let us sit with you, one at your right and one at your left.' When Jesus challenged them with what it might cost them they were quite confident; they could do anything, go anywhere, stand anything – it was worth it for the glory ahead, lording it over the rest of creation! They were promised a share in the experiences of Jesus, but not of those top places.

Of course the other disciples were furious when they heard what was going on. How dared James and John say such a thing? Was it, I wonder, that they had already allocated those roles to themselves in their minds, so resented the boldness of James and John in putting into actual words their desire for senior positions? Jesus got them all together and firmly and patiently reminded them of the true mark of greatness, that of service. Not a sort of 'public servant', which carried authority and respect, but a slave, the least of the least, being at everyone's beck and call, even of the other servants. Jesus did not ask them to do something he was not prepared to do himself, for his service cost him everything, even life itself.

Our church in Selby is dedicated to St James, and the east window depicts in the various panels the life of the apostle, the final one showing his execution. He did pay the price of discipleship, of being the servant of the servant of all; but even that was no guarantee of a senior seat in heaven, only of a martyr's crown, among the throng of faithful, obedient servants who had indeed lived and died in the steps of the Master.

I wonder how you see your service, what it entails? It is so easy to talk about being called to serve, being a servant of the Lord, when we still harbour illusions of grandeur. Recently I heard a sermon on 'Called to Serve', in which the preacher said, 'We so readily agree we are called to serve God, the trouble is most of us want to serve him in an advisory capacity only.' I don't know whether the preacher was being original, but it certainly gave me plenty to think about!

After Jesus had spelled out yet again to his disciples what following him entailed, I imagine it was a much subdued and more thoughtful group of men who travelled on with him, on to Jericho, where above all the clamour a voice was heard shouting for help. Not demanding, but pleading that Jesus would have pity on him. He was a blind beggar, and we are told his name, Bartimaeus. He had no claim on Jesus, no right to be heard, and the people around were quick to tell him that. He was told to shut up, in no uncertain terms. After all, he was nobody and nothing. But he was not to be put off; he carried on doing the only thing he could do, shout. To his joy Jesus stopped, and asked him to come to him. He could not move quickly enough, throwing off his coat so he could get to Jesus unhindered, and Jesus asked him the same question he asked James and John: 'What do you want me to do for you?'

Bartimaeus knew exactly what he wanted, his sight – and he had faith that Jesus could give it to him. His faith was rewarded immediately with the precious gift of sight. His eyes were opened to a new life, and his response was to follow Jesus, not for what he could get out of him, or in hope of position, but out of sheer gratitude. His name is recorded for all time, so that we may learn by his example. When Mark writes about the incident he names the man, probably because he became a well-known figure in the early Church. Mark could point to him and say, 'That man, the man you know, Bartimaeus, he is a living proof of the power of Jesus.' Bartimaeus, no longer a blind beggar but a servant of Jesus Christ. His eyes had been opened, not only to see the world, but to see the Saviour of the world, whom he would joyfully serve all his days.

That well-known and well-loved hymn 'Rock of ages' contains these words:

Nothing in my hand I bring,
Simply to thy cross I cling.
Naked come to thee for dress,
Helpless look to thee for grace . . .

It is the only attitude we can come with, not demanding our rights, but pleading for mercy, not with thought of position but wanting to see Jesus for ourself. History is strewn with those who looked for power and position, who gained it and lost it – as all earthly power must inevitably be lost. Your newspaper with today's date will contain details of power struggles, and of the failures of those who reach for power – try reading the business section! But the mercy and grace of the Lord will never fail us, his power will sustain us, 'his service is perfect freedom', for now and through to all eternity. That he does guarantee.

Lord,
I do my best to follow you, I want to be there with you, sharing in your glory, your victory.
Forgive me, Lord, but don't you think I deserve some sort of recognition for my dedication, my devotion to duty?
But there I go again, forgetting that without your grace I would not even know your name. Unless you had called me, I would be unable to serve you.
Have pity on me, open my eyes to your glory, that I may clearly see your kingdom. Open my heart and my will that I may serve you gladly all my days, all for love, as you have loved me.

Fit for a King

(11.1–11)

Everyone loves a procession, the bigger the better, and a royal one even more so. Several times in my life I have witnessed a royal occasion, been part of the cheering crowd, and had the thrill of seeing members of our royal family at close quarters, as well as other important dignitaries. Being part of a happy, excited crowd is a marvellous experience – the friendliness, the feeling of belonging, the shared sense of being part of something great. The word gets passed down the line, 'They're here!' Then the cheering comes to a crescendo, vying with the sound of the band, the clip-clop of horses' hooves on the road, and suddenly there they are, right in front of you, and your heart is bursting with pride and excitement as you strain to get a closer look, hoping to be rewarded by that eye contact, a smile, a wave, which you convince yourself is meant just for you. Afterwards the sense of achievement: 'I was there', something to tell and retell when it is all over, and tired and weary but still elated you make your way home again. It is a wonderful feeling, a highlight to be treasured, to be shared, even to the point of boring the family who have to hear your version of the day yet again!

When Jesus rode into Jerusalem on that first Palm Sunday, as it is known in the Christian calendar, everybody turned out to see him. Jesus' reputation had gone before him; the word had gone round, 'He's coming!' Everybody, it seemed, had a story to tell of the man who healed the sick, gave sight to the blind, some even said, raised the dead – and what a preacher, what a personality! There was more, though, to Jesus. It was said he was the Saviour they had been waiting for all these years, the one promised by God who would come to rescue them from oppression. With Jesus to lead them, soon they would know total victory over the dreaded Roman occupation forces, Jesus would show them the way to victory. Their troubles were over, for ever. It was all coming together in their favour at last.

For Jesus, it was all coming together. He knew the beginning and the end. This entry into Jerusalem was no impetuous decision done on the spur of the moment, but prayed through, thought through and no doubt wept through. He chose to come meekly and humbly, so that the people might grasp what his kingship, his kingdom was all about. He chose to ride on the colt which had never been ridden before, as a sign of sacred purpose, that he was coming not only in peace but to bring peace, the peace of God, not the victory of men.

Recently I saw on television a hardened general talking about an area of conflict he had been involved in, and he was being complimented on the success of the campaign, which he had spearheaded. Shaking his head gravely, he said, 'Any fool can start a war. It takes guts to finish one.'

Jesus was under no illusions as he rode into Jerusalem that day, with the crowd's cheers ringing in his ears, the acclamation, the branches spread before him, giving him what we call today 'the red carpet treatment'. Soon it would be truly red – blood red – his blood shed for the people of all time, of all nations, including you and me.

Jesus entered the city and went on into the heart of the city, to the Temple. What memories must have come flooding back as he again went into that holy place – memories of boyhood, of the joy of being there with his family, with friends, listening, learning, sharing. This place was for him his Father's house; he had come home again. Mark says so much in a few words, and never more so than when he records, 'Jesus entered Jerusalem, went into the Temple and looked round at everything' (verse 11). I find that sentence so poignant. In my mind's eye I can see Jesus standing there looking, just looking, and taking everything in. Nothing escaped his gaze, bringing memories of the past, the way it was at that precise moment and the knowledge of what was to come, for his people, his city, and that holy place. Having looked and seen, he braced himself, then turned away to join his disciples, and to spend the night in peaceful Bethany before returning the following morning again to his Father's house. He would have work to do then, but for the moment, for the night, he could be at peace, in quiet trust in his Father, who would provide the strength he would need. Tomorrow was another day, and as he had said to the crowd on the mountain, anxious about what was going to happen, how they could manage: 'Do not worry about tomorrow; it will have enough worries of its own' (Matthew 6.34). For now it was enough.

Lord Jesus,
When you rode into Jerusalem on Palm Sunday,
you knew it was the road to the cross,
yet you still took that road.
Give me the courage to take the road I should today,
whatever it may mean, wherever it may lead.
May I travel trustfully and obediently through this day,
content to leave tomorrow in your safe hands,
and tonight rest in your peace.

Promises, Promises
(11.12–14, 20–26)

At first reading this incident seems completely out of character for Jesus. To condemn a fig tree because it had no fruit, particularly as it was out of season, seems a petulant response arising out of disappointment – for the fig tree could hardly be blamed, could it? Jesus had never used his power to help himself – remember how he resisted the temptation to turn stones into bread? – and yet here he seems to be using his power in a negative and aggressive manner. We are told that Peter, the next day, drew attention to the dead tree. 'Look teacher, the fig tree you cursed has died.' Cursed? Can you imagine Jesus cursing anything or anyone? The event has been recorded for us by Mark, it must have been something that stuck very firmly in the mind, so what are we to make of it? One thing is sure, we cannot avoid it. It has been recorded, and recorded for a reason.

I cannot pretend to know the complete answer. I am not a biblical scholar in any sense of the word, but the more I read and think about it I realise that whatever the circumstances it did happen, and has a message for us. The tree was a disappointment to Jesus, holding out the promise of fruit without delivering it. Was it that Jesus used this experience as a visual aid for his disciples? As a sign of judgement upon those who promised so much, sent out all the right signals and then yielded nothing? Was it also a sign of what would happen to Israel, for all the professions of faith and service which had come to nothing? Was it a warning to those who would claim to follow Jesus and yet do nothing to show in their lives the reality of faith?

In Matthew's Gospel chapter 25, Jesus gives a warning of what happens when practice does not tally with profession. The girls who failed to provide oil for their lamps, the man who hid his master's money in the ground instead of being a good steward, producing a capital return. Those who failed to care for those in need: 'Away from me, you that are under God's curse . . . I was hungry but you would not feed me, thirsty but you would not give me a drink; I was a stranger but you would not welcome me in your homes, naked but you would not clothe me; I was sick and in prison but you would not take care of me' (Matthew 25.41–43).

The trouble with the fig tree was that at a distance it looked so inviting, full of promise, but it did not bear close inspection. It was an empty promise, and in spite of its attractiveness was worthless. Our runner beans were like that last year, a great disappointment, for after all, it was not the leaves or flowers we were interested in, but the end product; and there were no beans, so the plants were dug up and thrown on the compost heap. Figs, beans – but what about our lives? What about the promises we make to serve the Lord? Our frantic hurrying and scurrying round, organising this and that in the church, our names appearing as leaders, the hopes pinned on us, not just by people but by God. Where is the evidence of fruit being borne for him? In John's Gospel, Jesus says to his disciples, 'My Father's glory is shown by your bearing much fruit; and in this way you become my disciples' (John 15.8).

What have you or I to show for our faith in Jesus Christ? Where is the evidence? We need to think hard and long on this; after all, we are called to be faithful stewards of what God has given us. I always remember the words of a former Archdeacon of York when he talked of some Christians being 'spongers', soaking up all that God gives them but giving out nothing. 'Spongers' or disciples? – the difference lies in the end product. Jesus took the opportunity, though, to put the positive side of promises as he pointed his friends to the faithfulness of God. 'When you pray and ask for something, believe that you have received it, and you will be given whatever you ask for' (verse 24). God answers our prayers; he does not make empty promises, but provides for us all we need. He knows our needs better than we do ourselves, and can be trusted to meet them, even though sometimes we may not fully understand or accept that.

A verse from the book of Proverbs says, 'God keeps every promise he makes.' I have found in my life, in every circumstance, that this is true. He has never disappointed me, and the nearer I get to him, the deeper I enter into his life, then I find his promises unfolding like leaves in spring, and there at the centre the kernel which is his everlasting love – his promise fulfilled in me and for me. Draw closer to him now. You will not be disappointed. The closer you come, the more you will be able to receive, and the more you will have to share.

Lord,
Promises, promises. I make them so easily, and with so much confidence, but then what happens? They look and sound good, but is there anything really to show for them?
Am I like that fig tree, so full of importance and life, and yet yielding nothing?
Am I a disappointment to you?
I deserve your judgement, but I plead for your mercy. Renew me by the power of your Spirit that I may bring forth fruit for your kingdom, and live to your praise and glory.

By Whose Authority?
(11.15–19, 27–33)

It is a sad fact of life that there are always those who will take advantage of the vulnerability of their fellow men and women, who manipulate human need for their own ends. Some of us are old enough to remember the 'black market' in various goods and commodities during the Second World War, the 'easy pickings' of those who had a source of desirable goods and priced them accordingly. Only recently I saw scenes on television of desperate people being charged extortionate prices for food, profit being made out of frightened and starving refugees by human 'sharks'. Such conduct is bad enough in any circumstances, but when done under the cover of religion, trading on those who want to meet with God, it is an act of sacrilege.

When Jesus came into Jerusalem he came into a city thronged with pilgrims who had come from all over the world, travelling by long and arduous routes, beset with danger and deprivation. Many would have suffered illness and hardship, a considerable number would have been robbed, for highwaymen abounded on the pilgrim routes, and they would have been charged exorbitant prices for goods and services on the way. All this was forgotten in the joy of reaching the holy city, the fulfilment of a dream, the 'trip of a lifetime' – but only to be fleeced within the portals of the Temple. As the pilgrims exchanged their coins for the Temple currency they were cheated on the exchange rate. The doves which were to be offered for sacrifice were sold within a 'closed shop' belonging to the priest's family, again at an inflated price, from stalls set up in the very place where the pilgrims should have found a welcoming peace. Instead there was chaotic touting for custom and the culprits were the very people who should have been helping the weary pilgrims to come into a deeper experience of God. It was a system rotten to the core, deliberate greedy exploitation.

Jesus had seen it all; his searching gaze had missed nothing, and he was angry – angry because of the way these poor pilgrims were treated, angry because God's house had been desecrated.

Jesus strode through the Temple, overturning the tables, releasing the doves, moving out those who had so defiled that holy place. Quoting to them the words from the prophet Isaiah, 'The Lord says . . . my Temple will be called a house of prayer for the people of all nations' (Isaiah 56.7), he added his own condemnation: 'but you have turned it into a hide-out for thieves!' Of course, the Temple authorities were furious. How dare this Jesus judge them, insult them, and break up their very profitable business? Who did he think he was? Where did he get authority to interfere? After all, they were God's special people, they had the authority, not this self-styled rabbi from the backwoods of Galilee. Where were his credentials? Who gave him the right to make alterations in the running of the administration here? So they confronted Jesus with their angry and indignant questioning.

Jesus calmly turned the questioning on to them, pointed them back to John the Baptist. Was his authority from God or man? They were cornered. They knew that if they said 'from God', then the next question would be, 'Well, why didn't you believe him then?' If they said 'from man', the people who revered John as a great prophet would turn on them. So they gave the answer which so many

revert to when put on the spot, a plea of ignorance –
'We don't know.' They were not willing to listen,
not willing to admit they were wrong, and so Jesus
would not argue any further. Instead, he told them
a story, which we will think about in the next
chapter.

But before that, think about what happened in
the Temple and compare it with the life of the
Church today. What about the day-to-day running
of our ecclesiastical machinery, the way church
finances are handled, the question of fund raising,
our personal stewardship? Does it bring glory to
God? Is it done in such a way as to draw people to
God, to enable them to come closer to him, or does
it act as an obstacle? I know there are a million and
one ways of raising money for God's work, for the
upkeep of the church, for outreach. There is
straight giving, the garden fête, the bookstall and
the jumble sale, the stewardship campaign, the en-
velope scheme, the sponsored walk, the flower festival, and more and more and more . . . Never mind
the how, but the why. Not the practice but the
principle. If Jesus came into your PCC meeting,
your finance committee, when you were discussing
raising money to meet church expenses for the or-
gan, or the roof, or that new extension, or for the
missionary society, the homeless, the aid organisation, whatever, what would he have to say to you?
Be honest, really. Think about it. And whatever
you do, don't give the answer 'We don't know' –
because Jesus sees straight through that one, and
through us.

So often the Church is preoccupied with raising
money, seeking to tap new sources, by appeals to
the general public, frantic grubbing around for cash.
What comes over to those outside the Church is
'They only want you for what they can get out of

113

you'; or 'They are always after money.' The pilgrims who came to Jerusalem seeking God were obstructed by the commercialism and greed. How many of them returned home disappointed and disillusioned? What about those who today look longingly and hopefully to the Church for an answer to their problems, with a yearning for God, and are turned away by the constant emphasis on money? It saddens me as I visit churches and see that often the biggest notices are not of welcome but, 'This Church needs —— pounds', or 'Roof Appeal'.

Some years ago a visitor to our church in Selby, as he was leaving, shook hands with David, our vicar, and asked, 'Has this church any financial problems?' to which David answered, 'No, only spiritual ones.' I believe he had put his finger right on the spot, the heart of the question. Maybe Jesus needs to sweep through us, to come and challenge us, cleanse us, as he did in the Temple in Jerusalem. Perhaps it would do us good to be reminded again of his words, 'My Temple will be called a house of prayer for the people of all nations.' To recognise afresh that the purpose of a church is to be open and welcoming to all who seek God, and that his people should bear the cost willingly and generously. 'Cost' does not just involve money, it is far too important an issue to be reduced to cash, cheques or credit cards. It must affect our whole way of life, our attitude towards our fellow men and women, and our relationship with our God.

Lord,
Forgive us for being so obsessed with raising
money that we lose sight of the real purpose of
our church buildings. Lord, cleanse us, purify us,
remind us again of your great love, given freely

114

to us, and touch not just our hearts but our minds and wills and pockets, so that your house may be freely available for all who would enter, a haven of peace and joy, a meeting place with you, and a foretaste of heaven here on earth.

Called to Account

(12.1–17)

'Once upon a time . . .' four magical words which guarantee immediate interest. What a gift it is to have the ability to tell a story in such a way as to hold the interest and imagination of the hearers, to stretch them beyond the confines of a simple tale. Jesus was a great story-teller; he could, by using simple, familiar, everyday things and situations, portray great spiritual truths. We are told that he often spoke in parables, the word 'parable' coming from the Greek word *parabole* meaning 'a placing beside'. A parable invites us to make the comparison with our own experience. It is like being taken by the scruff of our neck and turned round to face up to what is happening here and now, and not just in a story about other people, another time. Fairy stories, fables, the world of pantomime are versions of this medium. It is a way of penetrating the guard of the hearer, and Jesus often used the parable for this very purpose, as he does in this parable of the tenants in the vineyard.

It was not 'an ordinary, everyday story of country folk' but concerned the love and mercy and the judgement of God. God gave man the privilege of sharing in this work of caring for the world, and he provided all that was necessary for the task; all he asked was for faithful stewardship. It was not forthcoming. He sent his prophets to remind them of what he expected of them; the response was to kill his messengers. God gave chance after chance, until finally he sent his own Son, believing he would be listened to, yet with the same result. After that there could be no further appeal, their privileges would be given to others. Jesus told the story to give his hearers, the religious authorities who had refused to accept him, the chance to realise the truth and do something about it. They got the point all right, but like the tenants in the vineyard they saw that their only way out was to destroy the evidence. One way or another Jesus must be silenced, and the sooner the better.

That parable was a prophecy, for it told of the rejection and death of God's own Son, a prophecy so soon to be dreadfully fulfilled. So while the religious leaders plotted and schemed, others, Pharisees and members of Herod's party, came to question Jesus. They too wanted him out of the way, and they thought they had found how to do it – a seemingly innocent and genuine question, but set at Jesus like a torch to a powder keg. The question of taxes. Should they pay taxes to the hated oppressor of God's people, Caesar the Roman Emperor, or not? If Jesus said Yes, then they could brand him as a traitor to his own people, and how could a traitor be from God? If he answered No, then they would report him to the authorities and he could be arrested for inciting to treason, the penalty for which was death. Jesus turned the question around to them by asking them a simple question, one they could not avoid: whose image was on the currency in use? They could not deny it was Caesar's. For whatever reason – that was not the question – Caesar ruled; he was sovereign over them whether they liked it or not, and taxation was part of his claim upon them. But Jesus added '. . . and pay God what belongs to God.'

That answer stands for every citizen in the world today as it did then. We are all subject to authority – 'No man is an island', as John Donne reminds us. We each have a responsibility to pay our way, to live in community, under authority. Just think about it, if we did not obey the laws of this land, there would be chaos and anarchy. As a citizen of this country I owe allegiance to it, I must take my part in protecting it, making my full contribution to its life; that is demanded of me. At the same time I am stamped with God's likeness, made in his image and redeemed by his Son, as Paul reminded the Christians at Corinth, and all who call themselves Christians: 'You do not belong to yourselves, but to God; he bought you for a price' (1 Corinthians 6.19–20).

God must take first place in my life. That is clear in the commandments given by God and confirmed by the words of Jesus, and I am required to show that in my life by what I do, what I say, how I think, my attitude to other people, every aspect of life. It must show as clearly in my life as the imprint on a coin. Living in this country at the present time I can carry my 'dual nationality' fairly easily, and I am thankful for that; but at the same time we all have to recognise that it is not so for many people in the world today. Many pay the price of their Christian discipleship through hardship, rejection, torture and imprisonment, and many already have paid with their lives.

As I look out from my comfortable position to what has happened and is happening I am challenged afresh to look at the image of my life. What do others see as I stand beside them at the supermarket checkout, in the bus queue, as we exchange greetings in the street? What about the conversations I have, the way I use my money and time, my response to people and situations in my own community? Have I dulled the image of Jesus Christ? Overlaid it with grime and muck, allowed it to be tarnished? I can only pray in words from Charles

Wesley's hymn 'Hark the herald angels sing':
'Adam's likeness, Lord, efface, stamp thy image in
its place' – and give constant attention to his claim
upon my life and seek by his grace to faithfully
serve him and reflect his image all my days.

Lord,
I hold a British passport, with a royal coat of
arms emblazoned on the front. There is my
name, the photograph is of me, and the signa-
ture is mine. I am proud of my citizenship, and I
want to bring honour to it.
Through grace I am a citizen of heaven. Not
through my effort, my place of birth, but be-
cause you love me so much you died for me, and
I proudly bear your name, I am a Christian.
Enable me to give you first place in my life, to
bear your image with joyful obedience, and at
the last to enter into your eternal kingdom,
where you reign for ever and ever. Amen.

More Questions

(12.18–37)

Some time ago I was in the company of a very learned and intellectual man who fired question after question at me. It soon became obvious to me that he was playing games, trying to catch me out on a technicality, rather like some of the 'Any Questions' type of programme. So I looked him straight in the eye and said very firmly, 'Most people ask questions because they want to find an answer. You are asking me questions because you believe you have the answers and I have not – so stop it!' He stared intently at me, his jaw dropped, and then he laughed. After that we got on very well, we understood one another, and were able to share in a genuine and open way.

The Sadducees were the 'crème de la crème' of Jewish society. They accepted only the written Scriptures, not all the traditions and customs so beloved by the Pharisees. The Sadducees consisted mainly of the most influential, priestly and aristocratic families, and their name is derived from 'descendants of Zadok' who was David's High Priest. Top people, all of them, and extremely influential. They accepted no concept of life after death; they were sure that death was the end, and so for them there was no such thing as heaven or hell, spirits or angels, life was entirely the here and now. So when they came to Jesus with a theoretical question about a woman who married seven brothers in turn and had no children, and whose wife would she be on the day of resurrection, it was not a real inquiry at all. They were trying to ridicule the teaching of Jesus, in effect to play games with him. Jesus cut through all that, dared to tell them they did not know the Scriptures – for they prided themselves on their knowledge of God – and then went in with the punch line: 'He is the God of the living, not of the dead. You are completely wrong!'

There are many Sadducees around today. They do not bear that name, but they follow the same tradition. They pride themselves on their position, their background, and their knowledge, while denying the love and power of God, and the reality of eternal life. They are not all outside the Church either. I am constantly amazed when I meet people who hold positions in the Church, are active in its affairs, and yet who have no belief in life after death, who quite bluntly say, 'When you're dead you're dead.' They love to have fancy arguments, getting themselves into print or on radio and television, and pontificating as though their views were the only ones possible for thinking people. I can only respond in the words Jesus used: 'You don't know the Scriptures or God's power' (verse 24).

The promise of life after death is clearly spelled out in Scripture, promised by Jesus and confirmed in his resurrection, and we will be dealing with that later in this book. But how tragic that the minds of the Sadducees were so closed. How tragic that minds of our present-day Sadducees are equally closed as well, to the glorious 'sure and certain hope' of the resurrection from the dead.

One man on the sidelines heard the discussion between the Sadducees and Jesus. He was a legal expert, and he had an open mind; he judged on the evidence before him and recognised the authority of Jesus, so his question was genuine, from the heart. He wanted to know which was the most important commandment. Jesus answered him with the summary of the commandments, duty towards

God and duty towards neighbour, all summed up in one word, 'love'. That was the key which opened up the law, for when we love someone we will want to please them, want to share, want to obey. It is not outward observance, protestations of obedience but that which springs up from the heart, the response of love, which is of more value than any sacrifice, or any other offerings. It was a genuine question, and the answer was understood and accepted. No wonder Jesus told the man he was not far from the kingdom of God. 'Not far . . .' there was something he still had to do, step out in faith with Jesus as his friend, teacher, saviour and Lord.

For us, too, it is not enough to ask questions, however genuine they may be, or to acknowledge that Jesus is the answer; there has to be the step of personal commitment to him. As we do that, and go step by step by faith, we will find the way becomes clear; for we are not alone, Jesus will walk with us, will share our life and bring us through all the perplexities and problems safely to his eternal kingdom. So many who heard Jesus thought only in terms of an earthly kingdom, earthly victory and success; they asked the wrong questions out of both criticism and ignorance. But the genuine seeker after truth always found the encouragement to go on seeking, for as Jesus promised: 'Ask and you will receive; seek and you will find; knock and the door will be opened to you' (Matthew 7.7) – and that is his promise to us as well, as if we really mean business.

Lord,
Thank you I can come with my anxieties, my questions, and my fears to you, and you will hear and answer me. Help me to listen, to accept and to obey, and to walk by faith in the light of your word day by day.

A Very Important Person

(12.38–44)

For days they had been busy clearing up. Every tiny piece of rubbish had been taken away, the edges painted, the grass verge trimmed. Then the tubs of flowers arrived, and the barriers were erected. Officials marched around looking very busy with pieces of paper in their hands, measuring, looking, checking yet again. Even more important-looking people arrived, including one who was definitely in charge; he had a bowler hat on - and gloves! A crowd of people had gathered. No one seemed to know what was going on, but obviously someone very special was expected. Then a large car drew up and a tall, rather distinguished-looking man got out, shook hands with several people, looked round for a while and then got back in the car and was driven away again. As the crowd drifted away, I overheard a man say, 'Well, I don't think he was anybody important, he'd got a mac on.' Actually the visitor was the Duke of Edinburgh! I think the man expected the Duke always went round in robes with a crown on his head; he didn't expect to see him dressed like any other man would be on a wet winter's day.

There is something within us all that equates outward appearances with degrees of importance. The expensive suit, the large hat, the loud voice, the demanding attitude, and we scurry round so easily taken in by appearances; and the confidence tricksters are quick to take advantage of this – so be careful! That was the warning Jesus gave about the teachers of the law who put on airs of importance, who strutted around dressed up in fine robes, and who demanded the best of everything. Those who made such a show of saying their prayers, who used their knowledge to defraud others, they were confidence tricksters all right, and Jesus said, 'Watch out!' Jesus saw through them, that it was all outward show; they were play-acting, 'hypocrites', there was nothing real about them. I sometimes wonder what Jesus would say if he saw some of the contortions the Church goes through at times, trying to prove how important it is. Is it real, bringing glory to God, or play-acting, putting on a show? I think we have to ask ourselves that. What are we about? Who are we trying to impress?

Last year at one of our family services our newly-formed group of Rainbows came to church, little girls of pre-Brownie age. It was obvious that for some of them church was a very new experience. After the service I was in the vestry taking off my robes when in came a couple of the little girls, wide-eyed, watching me. 'Is this your bedroom?' asked one. 'No,' I told her. 'Then why are you taking your clothes off?' I explained that these were special clothes I wore in church. 'What's church for?' asked the other one, looking very puzzled indeed. I tried to explain that the church was there so they could get to know about Jesus and come to love him. They seemed quite happy with the answer and skipped away. But I have pondered on their question many times: 'What is church for?' It is so easy to be over-concerned with the trappings that we forget who is at the heart of it all; we don't see the danger of the organisation taking over from 'the beauty of holiness', which should be our true offering in worship.

Jesus watched what went on in the Temple. Nothing escaped his penetrating eyes. He saw through those who made such show of their religion, he recognised the power-seekers, the self-important. He was not fooled then, and neither is he now. He had a scale of values based not on what seemed to be, but on what was real. When in the Old Testament story Samuel was sent to anoint the new king, God warned him against just looking at the biggest, the strongest and most important. He said, 'Man looks at the outward appearance but I look at the heart' (1 Samuel 16.7). Jesus saw the heart, the loving and generous heart, as he saw the poor widow putting her couple of coins in the offering box. Anyone else, had they even bothered to notice her, would have dismissed her and her tiny contribution, but Jesus knew it was all she had, and she gave it willingly, because it was for God. She would not have known who had seen her act of self-giving, that the commendation of her action would be recorded, and that she would be an example for all time. She was not concerned about gaining recognition or applause, it was a spontaneous act of love and joy. She was a very important person indeed, and will always be so. As for those who so proudly paraded their self-importance, they serve as a warning and a condemnation for all time too. And as Jesus said in the Sermon on the Mount of such people. 'they have already been paid in full' (Matthew 6.2). There is no more praise to come for them, ever.

Father,
Thank you for all you have given me, for life itself, for the promise of new life, for the joy of sharing in the lives of others and above all for being part of your life. In thankfulness and with love I give myself to you, all that I am, all that I have, and all I will be, for always.

The Shape of Things to Come
(13.1–23)

The city of York attracts visitors from every part of the world. It is very much on the tourist trail, helped, of course, by being at the centre of good communications, on the main railway line from London to Scotland. The 'jewel in the crown' of the city is York Minster, standing majestically in the centre, not only physically, but as the spiritual centre of the Diocese of York, and the 'mother' church of the Northern Province. Hallowed by centuries of prayer and worship, by splendid ceremonials, attracting the finest musicians, artists, craftsmen and women, it is breathtakingly beautiful. However many times I go into the Minster I am still moved by it, by what it stands for, its past and its present, by the sense of belonging I feel as I see it from afar, or from within its walls.

It is always a joy to share with other people the Minster's glorious history and also what is going on through that place today. I was talking to an American visitor recently who was completely bowled over by the sense of God's presence there. He said to me, with tears in his eyes, 'I've heard so much about this place, but nothing to prepare me for the experience I have had today. I will remember it for the rest of my life.' Then he added, 'It kinda puts the world into perspective, makes you realise that there is stability, timelessness, when you visit a place like this.' I agreed with him wholeheartedly, but tried to point out, however wonderful a building is, it can still be reduced to rubble – York Minster nearly was during the fire of 1984 – but God remains beyond buildings, beyond time and beyond us. He is eternal, the beginning and the end of all creation.

I can understand the feelings of the disciples as they looked at the great Temple of Jerusalem, that seemingly eternal centre of worship, that masterpiece of the finest materials and human achievement. They marvelled at it. They too were pilgrims rejoicing in actually being there in that holy place, and one of them put all their thoughts into words as he said, 'Look, Teacher! What wonderful stones and buildings!' The reply he got must have been a bombshell as Jesus said that every stone would be thrown down, that the Temple would be destroyed. It seemed an impossibility, and yet history proved it so. Within fifty years that proud building would be reduced to rubble, along with so much of the city.

As Jesus sat and looked at the Temple he must have been desperately sad, not just at the fact of what was to come, but that his city, his people, had rejected him. In fact he had cried out, 'Jerusalem, Jerusalem! You kill the prophets and stone the messengers God has sent you! How many times have I wanted to put my arms round all your people, just as a hen gathers her chicks under her wings, but you would not let me! And so your Temple will be abandoned and empty' (Matthew 23.37–38). Then, as he sat looking, four of his disciples, Peter, James, John and Andrew, came to him anxiously wanting to know when and how this was going to happen, and Jesus began to warn them of the trials and tribulations that lay ahead for all of them. It would be far more dreadful than the destruction of a building or a city, it would be the destruction of a people. Evil would seem to have total victory, and there would be terrible suffering, with no way of escape. For the followers of Jesus it would be even worse; they would be arrested, tried, betrayed even by their own loved ones, members of their families. They would be used as scapegoats, everyone would be against them, and it would seem totally hopeless.

Jesus did not mince his words; he had to prepare his disciples for what was to come, but how would they cope? Surely no one could withstand such suffering and horror! What could they say in the face of all this misery? What could they say when they saw the 'awful horror' – foreign idols set up in the Temple, the holy places desecrated? What could they say when other so-called Messiahs and prophets were acclaimed? What could they say when even those who professed to know Jesus were taken in by these people, captivated by what they were doing? What could they say in their own defence?

Jesus held before them the light, not at the end of the tunnel but in the blackness and despair of the tunnel, the light of the Holy Spirit who would enable them to share the good news, to speak boldly and plainly, to witness to the truth. They would not be on their own, they would be able to hold out because there would be someone to hold on to, and who would hold on to them, the Holy Spirit. Everything would happen as Jesus had warned them, but they would be ready, and they would stand firm because they would be empowered, just as Jesus had promised.

But this was not a situation that ended after fifty years, a hundred, a thousand or two thousand. It still goes on in our world of today, but now it seems even more horrendous, for it comes right into our living room day after day, through television. It drops through our letter box in our daily papers, it enters our day as we switch on the radio. For many

Christians it is even closer, they are engulfed by it. We may not be in areas of national suffering and upheaval, or personally taken to court for our faith, but suffering comes upon each one of us, in a multitude of ways – maybe through personal sickness and depression, family worries and conflicts, or through bereavement, isolation, or rejection. We are flung into the depths of our own feeling of inadequacy, our inability to cope with the questions that come from every side, the snide remarks, the cutting comments, and the accusing tone: 'Where is your Jesus now?'

William C. Lemmons in his book *Discovering the Depths* says this:

Our call to engage in a ministry of reconciliation with God to the brokenness in the world is a call to walk into that brokenness in the same manner Jesus did, and with the same lifestyle that guided him and the disciples after him. Ours is to minister and witness out of powerlessness and as servants. Then we will be accessible to the power of God through his Holy Spirit in all that we do.

And he continues, speaking of the Holy Spirit,

It would be a power for those who had decided that they no longer trusted in their own self sufficiency. It would be for those who had said they trusted God for their survival. The Holy Spirit would be for those who no longer could rest in their own strength when the waters got rough. He would be there for those who are demonstrating the staying power of faith, hope and love in the most difficult situations.

None of us knows what we will be called to go through, but we can know that, whatever it is, we can know the strength, the indwelling and empowering of the Holy Spirit. 'Hold out, hang on,' says Jesus. Here is our lifeline, which can never be broken, not even by death!

Come Holy Spirit,
fill me with your love,
your wisdom, your power.
Come Holy Spirit,
free me to serve,
free me to proclaim
Jesus is Lord
in all circumstances,
in all places,
and in all time,
and right now.
Come Holy Spirit, come!

But When?
(13.24–37)

The eager chattering ceases, the house lights dim, and all eyes are fixed on the curtain. Then comes the overture, a foretaste of what is to come. Suddenly the curtain rises, an explosion of sound and light and the star in all his dazzling, glittering glory appears to the tumultuous applause of the audience. He takes centre stage, gathering up the complete attention of every person present. This is what they have waited for, and he knows it. The timing is exactly right, everything has come together in unison; he commands, they joyfully abandon themselves to obey, to go where he takes them, to become part of that grand performance.

One day Jesus will take the centre stage. One day heaven and earth will bow to his command at the glorious 'second coming'. It will be the greatest 'Royal Command Performance' of all time, to which we are all called to witness. Just one thing – there is no date or time set. The prospect of the 'second coming' has captivated and challenged the heart of every believer from the time Jesus announced it until now. The Apostles' Creed proclaims, 'He will come again to judge the living and the dead' – but when? how? in what form? Eddie Gibbs in his book *Born into Battle*, commenting on Paul's letters to the Thessalonians, which deal in depth with the second coming, says,

This will be the greatest reunion of all times. It does not mean we will recapture the past with nostalgia, like a gathering of war veterans. Instead we will step together into a glorious and endless future. And heaven is not a place of countless cubicles, with each door marked 'private'. It is a place where Christians will be together and sharing with each other at far deeper levels than they have known on earth.

A wonderful prospect indeed, but we need to be ready at all times; it could be today.

At one of the main line stations in London, there is a huge billboard with the stark poster, 'Prepare to meet your God'. The commuters hurry by, so used to it they do not give it a glance. Tourists from the four corners of the world stream past, intent on enjoying the sights and sounds of London town; occasionally one will briefly look at that notice, maybe furrow their brows, smile, and go on their way. 'Prepare to meet your God' – they hope not, they have their own plans, their programme is not designed to include meeting god. No one takes seriously words like that.

And yet, can any of us guarantee that this day will come to an end before we are called to account? Jesus warms us that it will happen 'like a thief in the night', but do we take him seriously? The Advent hymns we sing so cheerfully are often seen as a prelude to the Christmas festivities, a reminder to 'post early', to order the gifts and cards, to book the plane or train seat, to stock up the cupboards with seasonal fare. Yet if we will take the trouble to look at those hymns we will soon realise they are speaking not of a preparation for Christmas, the celebration of Jesus' first coming as a baby at Bethlehem, but of his second coming in glory, 'to judge both the quick and the dead'. Charles Wesley's hymn based on Revelation 1.7, 'Look, he is coming on the cloud', reminds us:

132

Now redemption, long expected,
See in solemn pomp appear.
All his saints by men rejected
Now shall meet him in the air.
Alleluia, Alleluia, Alleluia,
See the day of God appear.

There will come the day when all creation will be gathered up and the final curtain will fall – a day of glory, a day of judgement, a day we must all face. We face it as belonging to Jesus, as his faithful servants; or else as outsiders, with nothing to plead, and certainly not able to plead ignorance. There is no escape, no back door, nowhere to run to but to be face to face with 'the king of glory'. Whether we believe that and feel it, or reject it and forget it, makes no difference. It will happen, Jesus said so. He has given us enough warning; it is up to us to act on his words. As he says, 'Heaven and earth will pass away, but my words will never pass away.' They stand firm for ever, and we answer to them for ourselves.

Lord Jesus Christ,
One day, it may be today, it may be tomorrow,
you will return, as you promised.
All will be revealed,
all will stand under your judgement.
May I be ready to meet you,
as my Saviour, my Lord and my King,
and be caught up to meet you
to be with you for ever and ever.
Amen.

What a Waste!
(14.1–11)

It was all rather embarrassing when you come to
think about it. Jesus is having a meal at a friend's
house when this woman comes in, walks up to him
and breaks a jar of very expensive perfume over his
head. Just imagine it, dripping down his head and
clothes, the smell of perfume wafting all over the
place; she must have been out of her mind, coming
in and doing such a thing, making such an exhibi-
tion of herself – and what a waste! That perfume
was the best you could get, worth a year's wages,
and she throws it away, gone in a few short moments. Why would anyone do something like that?
Obviously she wanted to give it to Jesus, but then,
why not have sold it, and presented him with the
money to help some of the poor people he met? She
had upset the meal, drawn attention to herself, and
created a sticky situation, in more senses than one.

Those in the house turned on her, but Jesus told
them to leave her alone. He said it was a fine and
beautiful thing she had done, she knew what she
was doing, she knew that Jesus was going to his
death because of his love for people like her, and
she wanted to show her love for him, her understanding of his sacrifice. And as for selling the perfume and giving the money away to the poor, you
can imagine Jesus turning and looking at those who
had suggested that: 'Well, have you helped them?
There are plenty of poor people around you, but
what have you done?' Yes, he had put his finger
right on a very sore spot, and they couldn't face up
to it. She did what she could, when she could, a
beautiful and costly offering, poured out in an

expression of total, spontaneous self-giving. It meant so much to Jesus at that particular time. Ahead of him lay betrayal, suffering and death. That act of love must have encouraged and strengthened him for what lay before him – and it would be remembered for ever.

One of my Christmas presents when I was twelve years old was an autograph book – all the rage at that time! My mother had written in it, 'You will pass through this world but once. Any good you can do, do it *now*, for you may never pass that way again.' It didn't make a lot of sense to me at the age of twelve, but over the years I have come to realise the truth of it. So often people say to me, 'If only I had . . .' Often this is said after the death of a loved one, a friend, a relative. The regrets of missed opportunities – and now it is too late. 'If only . . .' The story of that woman, the words in my autograph book, serve to remind me of the need to do what I can when I can – and sadly I often fail to heed the warnings, and I too re-echo the words, 'If only . . .'

I know how much impulsive acts of love mean to me – maybe a bunch of flowers, a phone call, a gift; love, like perfume, smells sweet, and lingers long. Maybe we need to act a bit more on impulse in life – it might cost us a lot, but it would make such a difference to others, who might just at that moment be in need of encouragement, needing to know they are loved and understood. 'What a waste', they said that day in Simon's house. Yes, there was a terrible waste, but not to do with the woman and her perfume; for read on, and see how one of those guests at dinner acted not on impulse but out of cold-blooded, calculating treachery.

Judas Iscariot, after seeing what that woman had done, after hearing his Lord's commendation of her action, went off to bargain with the chief priests, to put a price on Jesus. Having 'come to an arrangement,' he waited for the opportunity to cash in on it. What a waste! Judas wasted his life, his opportunities, threw them away, for what? Thirty pieces of silver. There are some things you cannot put a price on – love, integrity, friendship, honour. If only Judas had listened to what Jesus said! If only he had grasped what he was saying! If only . . .

What about the 'if onlys' in your life and mine. Never mind what the world things about us, it is what Jesus says that counts. What a tragedy if he had to shake his head sadly over us and say, 'What a waste!'

Lord,
May my response to your love come from a heart
set free from selfish desires, a sweet-smelling
sacrifice of praise and thanksgiving.

Celebrate for All Time
(14.12–31)

The Passover feast is the greatest festival in the Jewish calendar, a reminder and a celebration of the deliverance of the children of Israel out of Egypt – how God saved them from slavery and death to bring them into a new life, a new relationship with him, and into the promised land, the destination God had for his people. Not an optional celebration, it was clearly laid down in Exodus 12.14: 'You must celebrate this day as a religious festival to remind you of what I, the Lord, have done. Celebrate it for all time to come.'

So began the yearly celebration, and for everyone the great desire and hope was to be able to celebrate it in Jerusalem at least once in a lifetime. For adult Jewish males living within fifteen miles of Jerusalem, it was obligatory. So, as Passover time drew near, the road to Jerusalem would be crowded with people coming from near and far, like an English Bank Holiday on a hot summer's day. The crowds swarmed in, with every available room and space booked up. It was no use leaving it until the last minute. 'Book early to avoid disappointment' was a proven fact.

Jesus and his disciples were part of the crowd of pilgrims thronging Jerusalem. Jesus had made arrangements for them to be able to share together the sacred feast. There was nothing haphazard about Jesus, he had planned where it would be, but had said nothing to the others until the time came. Jesus needed privacy. He knew this would be the last time he would share the feast with his friends, he had much to say to them, to show them; so much hinged on this time together. Almost like a spy thriller, the clues were given, so the disciples could unobtrusively prepare the room and Jesus could quietly join them without attracting unwelcome attention. The questions we may well ask are: 'Who were these people who provided the cover? Why did the man allow his house to be used by Jesus and his friends?' All we can think is that they were supporters or believers, willing to help in whatever way they could. We do not know their names, but we thank God for their service which enabled that 'feast of feasts' to take place. They played their part, they were enablers in Jesus' ministry, a vital ingredient remembered for all time. Maybe we should remember that fact when we are called to do very ordinary things, the 'background' jobs which seem to have no real bearing on the kingdom of heaven. Let's remember the water carrier and the householder who were pieces in the jigsaw of eternity, of God's plan of salvation.

So it was that Jesus and his disciples sat to share that last meal, that sacred feast. Round the table were gathered those he had shared his ministry with over the last three years, those who would carry on the work after his death. One of them would soon be gone for ever – Judas. As they sat at table Jesus made the last appeal of love to him. Revealing that he knew what was going to happen, his words were a challenge to them all, but particularly to the one who knew it was him Jesus spoke of. Judas must have been scared – was Jesus going to tell the others? They would have killed him! What was going to happen to him now that Jesus knew? What happened was that Jesus shared his love and his life with Judas just as much as with the others. Judas had that last chance and he threw it away, and went out into the blackness, into despair, to death.

The meal that was shared was simple, bread and wine, but transformed by Jesus: 'This is my body' and 'This is my blood'. The bread and wine were visual aids of what was to happen, visual aids of the new covenent that the way would be open for all to come out of slavery, sin and death to new life, a new relationship with God and the assurance of an eternal future with him.

In my book *The Cost of Living* I wrote of that feast

It has been the inspiration of artists, musicians and writers. It is seen as a symbol of love and unity and also of division and rejection. The wise and learned seek to explain it, the humble accept it with awe and wonder. It is re-enacted wherever the name of Jesus Christ is known. As you read this, men and women in many different places and circumstances will be taking part in the portrayal of what happened two thousand years ago in an upper room in Jerusalem.

It has been given many names: the Lord's Supper, the Eucharist, Holy Communion, Mass, Breaking of Bread – the name does not matter so much as what we experience. We in our day and in our way share bread and wine, as we obey the command of our Lord to 'do this in remembrance of me'. As we receive by faith what Jesus has done for us, as we take into our bodies and our souls the bread and wine, his body, his blood, we are reminded of his saving grace, that we are part of the new covenant.

As we come with others, we share with a wide variety of humanity; no two of us are alike. We all have our strengths and weaknesses, our fears and and failings, courage and hope. We are all capable of great things, and equally we are all capable of the lowest. but Jesus invites us to come, to be his guest, to share the feast. 'The Lord says, come!' All he asks is that we accept his invitation to take from him what he offers, and allow his life to change us, strengthen us, encourage us to be what he wants us to be. Judas took and then turned away. I cannot but feel desperately sorry for Judas, his was the greatest loss of all time. If only he had turned to Jesus and asked for forgiveness, he would have received it, no doubt of that.

Judas was not the only failure in that room. They were all failures one way and another. The difference was that the other disciples would accept forgiveness and start again. Even Peter, who would find it impossible to forgive himself for a time, would discover the limitless love of his Lord and Master, and become the rock Jesus named him.

As the eleven disciples went out of the room to the Mount of Olives with Jesus they were reminded again of what was going to happen. They would run away, Peter would deny his Lord, even before the cock finished crowing. But there was the promise for the future: 'But after I am raised to life I will go to Galilee ahead of you,' said Jesus. They would not walk into the darkness like Judas, but into the light, the light of the Lord's presence, of reunion and re-commissioning. That is the promise for us, too.

Sweet feast of love divine,
'tis grace that makes us free
to feed upon this bread and wine
in memory, Lord, of thee.
O, if this glimpse of love
is so divinely sweet,
what will it be, O Lord, above
thy gladdening smile to meet. (E Denny, 1839)

Lord,
You bid me come to the feast,
knowing my failures,
knowing my weakness,
knowing everything about me,
yet you still invite me.
I do not deserve to be invited,
I would not dare to presume to come,
but in those symbols of bread and wine
I see your love for me, even me.
Lord, with joy I accept your invitation,
Lord, I come to your table,
I come as your guest,
I take and eat, I take and drink,
and in your life I am made new.

Who Needs Friends?

(14.32–42)

When Jesus set out on his ministry he chose twelve men to share his life and his work. 'I have chosen you to be with me,' he told them. Jesus, who was both man and God, needed and wanted human companionship as he needed and wanted his heavenly Father's companionship. In Jesus we see that wholeness of life that is a pattern for our lives, too. Jesus had the balance exactly right; nothing would come before his relationship with his Father. That is why he got up early to spend time alone in prayer. That is why he made sure he had that regular time away from people. He needed that close, regular communion with God his Father. It was because his friends saw what that meant to him, that they asked him to teach them to pray. They saw that prayer worked. They saw the effect of that closeness of Father and Son.

But Jesus also enjoyed human company. One of the criticisms levelled against him was that he ate and drank with ordinary people, that he was seen in the company of those the religious leaders considered sinners and beyond the pale. He enjoyed visiting friends, sharing meals in their homes. He was no name-dropper but a 'people-picker-upper'.

His twelve disciples were special friends. They shared his life day by day, and with them he shared his ministry, his ideals, his plans. Within that group there was an inner circle: Peter, James and John. To them he revealed the deepest longings and aspirations of his life. He took them into the very heart of his being.

As I look at my life I delight in my friends and thank God for the immense variety of them, for their love and friendship over so many years, the fun we share, the situations we have been through together. I have been blessed with many friends, but I know that within that circle of friendship there are special people with whom I share my life at a much deeper level; and I can count on one hand those who are extra special, with whom I can be totally myself, reveal my heart, and to whom I can turn for help, guidance and support. I know that any time of day or night they would answer, I feel I can depend on them one hundred per cent. I trust them and I love them, and they, I believe, trust and love me. But I know they are human as I am human; we could fail each other, it is possible – and who knows what would happen if we were put to the test in circumstances yet unknown. I know this, though, it would break my heart if I failed them or they me; but I am a realist, and I see failure under pressure in many situations, so who can really judge until they are in such a situation themselves?

Peter thought he could. In fact he was sure he could. He took it very badly when Jesus told him that he would fail, and run away. Peter could not accept the possibility – all right, others maybe, but not him; he would die first.

Jesus took his little inner circle, Peter, James and John, into Gethsemane, that oasis of peace and quiet, which was to be his last chance of being alone with his friends. Jesus knew what lay ahead, suffering and death, rejection – could he face it? He was a young man in his prime, only thirty-three, strong, wise and so much to give – but life itself? Was that too much to give? He had to battle it out, he had to know beyond doubt that this was the only way. He knew his Father could save him, but should he? If this was the only way, then his will must be in tune with his Father. But it was hard. There were so many reasons why he should not go through with it. After all, who in their right mind walks voluntarily into such a situation if there is a way out?

Jesus is torn – he needs his Father, he also needs, more than he has ever needed before, his friends. Not to rescue him, not to talk to him, not to do anything but be there, to watch and pray – to pray for him, to pray for themselves that they might be equal, by God's grace, to whatever might come.

Desperately Jesus prays, asks his Father to take the cup of suffering away; but in obedience he also prays, 'Yet not what I want, but what you want.' He went through agony in his prayers. Luke's Gospel account says, 'His sweat was like great drops of blood falling to the ground.' A man sweating out his destiny, the conflict wringing him out like a sponge, and his friends, watching and praying, supporting him in his desperate need – no, they were asleep! Imagine the bitter disappointment as he finds them deep in sleep, uanware of his struggle. He pleads with them, 'Keep watch and pray,' but he knows that for all their good intentions, they are weak. Again he prays, again they sleep, and they are so embarrassed, they cannot say anything. The final time he prays, and returns to find them asleep again. No use now, it is too late, they have failed him in his hour of need, and he can already hear the sound of the approaching crowd, coming to take him away. The friends have lost their battle with sleep, but Jesus has won his personal battle – he knows his Father's will, and faces up to it. What a tragedy, what a disappointment, that he had to do it alone.

Jesus needed his friends' support – they failed him through weakness of body. But worse is to come. Now he is betrayed, cold-bloodedly sold for a handful of silver; and the three failures look into the face of the betrayer, Judas – the one they also had trusted. He too has failed his Master, and his failure, deliberate, planned and executed, is the kiss of death to Jesus. As a modern expression has it, 'Who needs enemies when you have friends like these?'

Lord Jesus,
It is easy for me to judge the weak-willed friends, the cold and calculating traitor, but I have never been put in their position. I don't know how I would behave. Lord, help me to watch and pray, to be faithful to my friends, and above all to you, my Saviour and my friend.

The Observer Observed
(14.43–72)

They moved in quickly to arrest him. Once the signal was given, Jesus, marked out by the traitor's kiss, was pinned down. There was a scuffle, an exchange of blows between the supporters of Jesus and those of the High Priest, and it was over in the space of moments. The disciples ran for their lives, and we are told that one young man – it could have been Mark, it seems it may have been – had his clothes wrenched from him as he fled in terror. Jesus was hauled off to be brought before his accusers. Alone, all his friends had disappeared – or had they? One, Peter, followed at a distance, hiding in the shadows, mingling amongst the crowd, head down, but ears straining to hear what was going on.

It was not good. Jesus stood accused by so many. There were those who would eagerly testify against him, contradicting one another in their efforts to damn him. It was all confused, garbled. The High Priest knew he could not bring a conviction against Jesus on the evidence of such people, much as he wanted to. And in all the noise, the shouting, the threatening, Jesus stood silent. He would not enter into it, until the fateful question, 'Are you the Messiah, the Son of the blessed God?' Jesus could not but speak the truth: 'I am.' He affirmed his Sonship, and told what was to come on the day he would return in glory.

Jesus had played into their hands by that statement. To them it was blasphemy, he was condemned out of his own mouth. No need now for witnesses, no need for paid accusers, Jesus was finished, he had in effect signed his own death warrant. That was the moment they had waited for, and they made the most of it. Spitting, hitting, slapping, insulting him, they were the victors, Jesus the victim, and they would make him suffer for it, he was in their power.

. . . And what about Peter? Moment by moment getting more agitated, angry, frightened, yet unable to do anything. Should he rush in, could he rescue Jesus? What could one man do? The answer was nothing, and that is what he did – nothing, apart from staying within earshot. But then trouble. In the flicker of the firelight where he sits warming himself, a girl looks across, recognising him as one of those who had been with Jesus, and says so. Peter tries to bluff his way out: 'I don't know what you are talking about,' he says and tries to slide away, backing into the passage. The girl is insistent, she points Peter out to others: 'He's one of them.' Petrified, Peter denies all knowledge. But by now he has aroused the interest of those around; they have recognised his accent, he is a man of Galilee all right, he cannot disguise the fact. And Peter, blind with panic and confusion, swears he has never met the man Jesus, it is nothing to do with him! – and in that moment, above all the shouting, the argument, the denial of the truth, comes the sound of the cock crowing. Peter is stopped in his tracks, the fear and anger instantly replaced by terrible remorse, as he remembers what Jesus said, 'Before the cock crows twice tonight, you will say three times that you do not know me.' The seemingly impossible has happened, Peter is a total failure, he has failed himself, he has failed his Lord, and he is a broken man.

How could Peter have done such a thing? Peter, the member of the inner circle of friends of Jesus. Peter who was so brave, Peter older than the others, who should have known better. Peter the coward, Peter who sank so low as to curse and swear he had never even met Jesus, let alone been his friend. Peter, the one Jesus had named 'the Rock', was nothing but a mess of quivering jelly, useless, totally useless.

Maybe there is something in us which is quite relieved to read what happened to Peter that night. After all, if he could be such an abject failure, and still be restored, then maybe there is hope for us. But there is more to it than that. Just think for a moment. Who told Mark about that incident? Was there a witness who made sure everyone knew what a rotter Peter was, what a failure? I believe it was Peter himself who shared with others that dreadful failure, who openly confessed his cowardice. Not for pity, not to shock, but as an example, his own living example, of the danger of pride, of trying to 'go it alone' and failing miserably; but wonderfully demonstrating that someone who had done that could be given a second chance, could be accepted, loved and recommissioned.

That is exactly what did happen. Jesus, later, after he had risen from the dead, came to Peter in love, understanding, forgiveness and acceptance. More than that, he gave him a position of authority, of trust, and Peter's awful experiences that dreadful night did not weaken him but strengthened him. He did become the Rock, he did fulfil his Lord's commission. He took his second chance with both hands, and this time he did not fail.

We all fail, but the danger is, we may be content to wallow in our failure. Failures become compounded, and we give up, but Jesus never gives up on us, his hand is always outstretched to raise us up, to bless, to heal, to strengthen. The question he asks of us is the same he faced Peter with: 'Do you love me?' (John 21.15). In fact he asked Peter that question three times, to enable Peter to affirm his love threefold, so that he would know his threefold denial had been dealt with for all time.

Three times? How many times do you fail, do I? Many, many times. But Jesus understands our weakness, our failure and our guilt. He knows, too, whether we love him or not; and love of course is the key to understanding. 'Do you love me?' I hardly dare answer, but I can only say as Peter did, 'Lord you know everything, you know that I love you' (John 21.17) – and he does know, and that is what really matters in the end, isn't it?

Lord,
As I read of Peter's failure to live up to his prom-
ises, of his weakness when he was so sure of his
strength, I see myself. I remember the promises I
have made and failed to keep, through neglect,
thoughtlessness and fear. Like Peter, I weep
when I realise how often I have let you down.
But I know you went on loving him, you picked
him up and gave him another chance to be the
person you intended him to be. You called him
the Rock, and you enabled him to be that rock.
Thank you that day by day you go on loving me,
picking me up, giving me another chance.
Lord, I do love you,
and I know you know I do.
Thank you for loving and knowing me,
please strengthen me that I may serve you
faithfully
to the end of my days.

The Choice is Yours

(15.1–15)

Pontius Pilate's name is well known to everyone who has ever recited the Creed. The great affirmation of Christian faith includes the name of the Roman Governor who allowed himself to be manipulated into passing sentence of death upon Jesus. Pilate had no time or sympathy for the Jews, and he certainly did not want to be mixed up in their religious arguments, that was their business. He was there to keep order, to make sure they were kept in their place, and if possible for him to have a quiet life. He was no fool, he knew all about Jesus, and in fact felt attracted to him. He saw the difference between the so-called religious leaders and the one who seemed to have real authority.

So Pilate was not happy when faced with confrontation, and as the chief priests bombarded Jesus with accusations, Pilate looked to Jesus to answer them, to speak up in his own defence. Why didn't Jesus speak? Didn't he know it was a matter of life and death? Had Pilate known the words of the prophet Isaiah, about the 'Suffering Servant' (chapters 52 and 53), maybe he would have understood the significance of the silence. The accusers knew the Scriptures all right, but their minds and hearts were blinded to them. No doubt they could recite them word perfect, but those words were mere words to them; and remember, even the devil could twist Scripture, for instance when he tempted Jesus in the wilderness. The devil and men have used Scripture to their own advantage on many occasions, and still do!

Pilate was cornered, and he knew it. The chief priests were too clever for him, they were stirring up trouble. Should there be a riot, and it looked as if it was going that way, it would do his career no good; news would get back to Rome, and his days of peace and quiet would be over. There was a solution, though. As a favour, each Passover time Pilate released a prisoner as a sop to the people, a sign of good will, a piece of public relations. It still happens in our world today – men's lives are used as political currency, an exchange rate in blood.

Pilate was holding a bandit named Barabbas, a violent and fanatical nationalist – you would say their equivalent of Robin Hood, but much nastier, and much more real, a menace to society in general and the government in particular. So Pilate gave the people their choice. He would release Jesus or Barabbas, it was up to them. Did they want Jesus at large, going about his ministry of preaching, helping and healing, or Barabbas set free to continue his work of violence, murder and insurrection? But the chief priests were one step ahead of Pilate, and stired up the crowd, no doubt appealing to their sense of nationalism. Barabbas stood against law and order, against the Romans, that was in his favour; he was a destroyer, he lived by the rule of terror, that appealed to many in the crowd that day. Jesus stood for peace, for forgiveness, for honesty and holiness. Barabbas' way was the rule of force, Jesus' the rule of love. The chief priests, the crowd and Pilate chose the easy way out, and chose Barabbas. Mark says that Pilate wanted to please the crowd. He succeeded, and in so doing entered the pages of history and eternity as the one who passed sentence on Jesus. In so doing he passed sentence on himself.

A crowd-pleaser, a man who wanted an easy life, who wanted to avoid trouble at any cost – that was Pilate. There have been many Pilates throughout history. Their names are scattered through the history books and in the newspapers on the stands today. It is easy to despise them, to condemn them, but isn't there a bit of Pilate in us all? I know I try to avoid trouble. There are times when I play to the gallery, and let things go that I know I shouldn't because I don't want to get involved, or put myself in a difficult situation. My own skin, reputation and time come first.

We are told in Matthew's Gospel (27.24) that Pilate washed his hands publicly in front of the crowd to show them in that visual way that he was washing his hands of the situation: 'I am not responsible for the death of this man! This is your doing!' As if doing that released him from responsibility! It was a useless gesture, the gesture of a frightened man, of a man who knew what he was doing, and yet for fear of what others might say or do went against what he knew to be right.

What sort of gestures do you and I make? What clever arguments do we put forward to excuse ourselves? What use are they in the end? What answer can we give to God when we are called to account? These are serious questions we do well to attend to – while we have time.

Father,
Life is full of choices,
and I am called to make them day by day.
Choices that affect my life, my home,
my family, my future.
Choices that affect other people too.
Choices that will determine what
happens in their lives.

152

Like ripples on a pond,
spreading outward,
so my decisions form the direction
of the ripples of life.
I can please myself,
please others
or please you.
Help me to get it right.

What Would You Have Done?

(15.16–20)

I'd seen him earlier as I made my way – with five thousand other people – into the theatre. The policeman was young, fresh-faced and blond, with a slightly arrogant air about him, the 'on duty look'. He was there not to see the play but to keep an official eye on the audience. Mind you, what sort of trouble were we likely to cause at the Oberammergau Passion Play? But then you never know, there had been all that business of forged tickets, and there had to be someone to enforce the no smoking, no photographs rules. We settled down in our seats, the Red Cross discreetly by the entrance to deal with anyone who felt ill, or to help with the folk in wheel chairs at the front. The door stewards, their duty done, went out of sight around the corner, and the play began. People around me faded into insignificance, apart from those on the open air stage, with its natural backcloth of mountains, trees and sky.

Just before the start of the second half of the play I noticed the policeman again. There was, slightly over to my left, a raised platform running down the side of the theatre, a vantage point, and he was walking along it, every now and again glancing across the audience, casting his trained eyes over us. As the play resumed I noticed he had settled himself down, almost out of sight, head down; maybe he had a good book to pass the time until his spell of duty was over, or perhaps he was writing his report. As the play gathered momentum I forgot everything but what was going on on stage, the events leading to the crucifixion. Then we came to the actual crucifixion, three men to be executed, two thieves and Jesus. The coarse laughter, mocking homage, abuse and thud, thud, thud of the nails. The crosses hoisted into position, then the soldiers playing dice at the foot of the cross on which Jesus hung. It was like stepping back two thousand years, being there, and I wondered, 'What would I have done?'

Then for no reason I know of, I looked up to my left. The policeman was there, standing erect, gazing at that scene. He looked almost in pain, tearful, and I could see his knuckles were white as he gripped the top of the rail. Was he, too, thinking what he would have done in those circumstances? After all, those soldiers putting Jesus to death were just doing their job like him, keeping law and order. Young squaddies, in uniform, trained to sort out crowd trouble, to deal with trouble-makers like the man they were making sport of. What would the young policeman have done in their position?

Anyway, what could he have done? Perhaps been a bit less abusive to Jesus, maybe a 'Sorry mate, but it's my job'; or would he have enjoyed making the prisoner suffer more, a bit of entertainment to make the time go quicker as a member of the execution squad?

Whatever was going on in his mind and heart, he was totally taken up with the events being played out before him, and by his expression it was no mere performance he was witnessing; he was there, and struggling to understand his own emotions. As I looked at him he suddenly looked down at me, knew I was watching him, and our eyes met. It was as though we were the only two people in that theatre, and we were saying to each other 'Well, what are you going to do about him?' It must have lasted only seconds, but it seemed like hours. Then

I looked away at Jesus on the cross, and watched his agony, his death, then all was darkness, silence, followed by thunder, lightning, shouting.

At the end of the play the crowd streamed out. I followed the others, and waiting to cross the road I saw a young blond policeman directing traffic. He smiled at me as I passed him. Was it the same one or not? They all looked alike in uniform, as I suppose all tourists look alike to them, wandering along, clogging up the streets; and the police have a job to do, directing traffic, keeping the people moving in the right direction, making sure everything goes smoothly, trouble free, nice and tidy-like . . . Maybe that's what the soldiers had to do two thousand years ago when they were on execution duty, keep it all tidy, under control, moving along. I wonder, after it was all over, did they give Jesus another thought, or was it all just another day's work? And what about that policeman in Oberammergau – does he ever think back to that day on duty in August 1990, when an age-old story became suddenly intensely personal? I know this, I will always remember it, and I pray he will too.

Lord,
Help me in the ordinary everyday duties of life to recognise you and acknowledge you as Saviour and King, and fashion my life according to your example of love and sacrifice.

The Conscript
(15.21–32)

Just after the Gulf War I saw a most disturbing piece of film shown on the television news. It was of a public execution in Kuwait during the war. Filmed secretly from a window, hidden away until it was safe to reveal it, it showed three nameless men being executed by firing squad. A silent crowd stood watching. A small boy on a bicycle rode past, seemingly unconcerned, and a large military presence stood by as the executions were carried out. After it was all over the crowd dispersed, the soldiers left, and the three bodies remained in the square – end of film. I have thought about that scene many times since. Will those who witnessed it remember that day, I wonder? Will it have affected their lives, their ideas, changed their attitudes or allegiance?

I think of another public execution of three men, Jesus and two thieves. Watched by a crowd, surrounded by a military presence, carried out by an execution squad. There were those there that day, witnesses, whose lives were changed by being present, and one was Simon of Cyrene. As he had left his home in Africa on the journey of a lifetime, a joyful journey to be in Jerusalem for the Passover, he could have never imagined the nightmare he would be caught up in, made to share in. There he is, going along with the crowd, and a hand comes on his shoulder, he is dragged out from the crowd by a couple of tough-looking Roman soldiers, into a terrifying procession. Two condemned men are staggering along under escort with huge wooden crosses on their shoulders. They are on their way to be crucified, the most barbaric form of execution devised by man. Another man lies on the floor, unable to get up; he has been badly beaten, he looks half dead already, and although he is yelled at, and kicked, he cannot move his wooden burden. Simon realises why he has been pulled out. He has to stand in for that man, he is press-ganged to carry the execution block.

Can you imagine how Simon felt? He must have been petrified – was he to be crucified too? There was no mercy shown by these Roman oppressors, no one to appeal to. He shouldered the cross, and joined that ghastly procession winding its way to the appointed place of execution. Having got to Golgotha the soldiers let Simon go, he had served his purpose. Everything in Simon made him want to get away as fast as he could, away from the nightmare, but something kept him there. There was something about the man whose cross he had carried; he was different, he was no criminal, Simon could see that. So why was he being executed?

The soldiers set about their business. There was the sound of the nails being driven in, the coarse laughter as they heaved up the three crosses into an upright position. There were the cries of pain and terror, the screaming, insults and curses being hurled by the two thieves at their tormentors and also at the man in the middle, the man whose cross Simon had carried. There was a noisy, aggressive crowd there too; most seemed in agreement with the soldiers, and Simon noticed that amongst them were chief priests and teachers of the law. A strange place for them to be! Even stranger that they, as men of God, should be insulting a dying man. Everyone seemed against that man in the middle, the man they called Jesus. Sneering, taunting, shouting, 'Come down from the cross and save yourself!' – as if he could! It was a noisy, nasty business, highly charged emotions erupting into a strident discord of almost unbearable volume. As the time went by the priests and teachers seemed to get even more angry as they yelled at Jesus, commenting to each other almost hysterically, 'He saved others, but he cannot save himself! Let us see the Messiah, the king of Israel, come down from the cross now, and we will believe in him!' Yet in all this the man in the middle, the one they called 'the Messiah', was dying, painfully, horribly; but unlike those on either side of him there was no cursing, no shouting, but he seemed to be praying, praying even for those who were doing this awful thing to him, actually praying for those who cursed him, who laughed at him, who had nailed him there.

Simon knew there was something special about that man. He was a good man. He was . . . well, who was he really? Whatever happened that day it changed Simon. We are told he was the father of Alexander and Rufus, and Paul writing to the Romans several years later says, 'I send greetings to Rufus, that outstanding worker in the Lord's service, and to his mother, who always treated me like a son' (Romans 16.13). Simon and his family had become believers, followers of the man in the middle, Jesus the Messiah, the one who was the Saviour of the world, the Saviour of Simon, his family and of millions on millions of others from that day to this.

Press-ganged into service that fateful day, 'in the wrong place at the wrong time' – and yet it was the day Simon's life was changed eternally by what he experienced. At the time it seemed the worst day he had ever experienced; looking back, he could thank God for that day, when he met his Saviour, when he found new life through what happened on that cross. Frank Colquhoun, in his book *Strong Son of God*, says of that encounter:

> At the time Simon little knew what it meant. But who can doubt that in after years he looked back to that day with ever deepening gratitude? What had seemed to him at the time a burdensome duty imposed upon him by the Roman soldiers he came to regard as his highest privilege. For he came to learn that on the very cross he carried to Golgotha the Son of God bore away his sins – and the sins of the whole world.

There are times in life which we would rather forget – experiences which leave us battered, confused, and diminished, or so it seems. 'Why me?' we cry, and there comes no answer – at the time. Paul, writing to the Romans, says, 'We know that in all things God works for good with those who love him, those whom he has called according to his purpose' (Romans 8.28). I can look back in my life and see events and circumstances which at the time made no sense, which seemed totally negative, and yet as I look at them now I realise how much good God has brought out of them for me. I hang on to that verse, I know the reality of it. Simon 'hung on' to his eternal salvation. Jesus hung on that cross, for yours and mine. It has been said that 'it is not the nails that kept him on the cross, but love.'

> Bearing sin and scoffing rude,
> in my place condemned he stood,
> sealed my pardon with his blood,
> Halleluia! What a Saviour!　　　*(P.P. Bliss, 1875)*

Father,
Sometimes I question why certain things hap-
pen to me.
Why should I have to go through this?
Why don't you do something?
Why me?
Perhaps Simon said, 'Why me?' that day he was
picked out of the crowd.
'Why me?' when he was made to shoulder that
heavy load,
'Why me?'
It was nothing to do with him was it?
Yet there he met Jesus,
he found his Saviour,
he came into new life.
In life's experiences may I discern your hand
working for good, and in all things may I dis-
cover more of the love and power of Jesus my
Saviour, who suffered and died that I may know
the joy of eternal life. I ask this in his name.

Darkness and Light
(15.33–39)

Jesus hung on the cross, his life ebbing away, bit by bit, drop by drop. Excruciatingly in agony he hung there for all to witness his defeat, his humiliation, his rejection. It was a black day, the powers of darkness had triumphed. Even the elements turned black, the day eclipsed by night; darkness covered the whole country, in mourning for the one who hung not only in the dark, but in black despair. He cried out to his Father, his God, 'My God, my God, why did you abandon me?' The cry of dereliction. That was for him the greatest anguish – that God had after all forsaken him, given him up. Everything was black, blacker than the blackest night.

What can I say about that moment? Only perhaps recognise something of that blackness, that 'dark night of the soul'. But no one can really enter into that moment. Jesus, the sinless one, the one who had such a close relationship with his Father, who had always obeyed his Father, now feels separated, deserted. The other Gospel accounts record other words he spoke, but surely these words plumb the depths of his suffering. We know the story so well, we are used to the symbol of the cross; perhaps that very familiarity lessens the reality of the cost in suffering that Jesus went through on that black day.

During Holy Week a couple of years ago we held a service in church for the children of the school where my vicar David and I go each week to take assembly. Part of the service took the form of a Passion Play put on by the children, and one young lad had the job of standing holding the cross. A jolly, lively boy, always on the go, for that time he stood quite still, holding the cross. Afterwards he came up to me looking very solemn, almost tearful in fact. 'Mrs Cundiff, do you know what they did to Jesus? They put nails in his hands and nails in his feet.' He looked down at his own hands and feet, then blurted out, 'I bet it didn't half hurt!'

That little lad understood what the cross was all about, the awful price Jesus paid. His young open mind had not been cluttered up with pretty images, well-worn theologial arguments, it was real for him, and he felt for Jesus at that moment. No wonder Jesus said we all need to be as little children, for children have the gift of recognising the heart of the matter, and are not afraid to look, not afraid to put their reaction into words. I know this, that little lad's comment has given me a fresh awareness just of the suffering, physical, mental and spiritual, which Jesus endured on the cross. It did hurt, and the hurt went into his very soul.

Yet in all that suffering the light of truth pierced through the darkness, and those who were prepared to see received the light. One of them was the Roman officer in charge of the execution. He must have done many such duties – it was all part and parcel of life as an officer in the army of occupation. He had to stand there until it was all over, until he was sure the convicted men were dead, and then write up the 'job completed' form, the death certificate. He, who had witnessed death so many times, saw in the dying of Jesus on the cross that 'this man was really the Son of God!' Who knows what resulted from his experience as he shared his discovery with his fellows?

Some, of course, listened to Jesus with idle curiosity. They watched him die, wondering if something might happen, some sensational activity they could gape at – they were disappointed. Had they been in the Temple they would have seen an amazing happening; the curtain which shut off the Holy of Holies was torn in two as Jesus died. Only the High Priest could go beyond that curtain, and that once a year on the Day of Atonement; it was not for ordinary people to go into the presence of God. Now the way was opened for all and it is open for all time. God is not distant, not hidden; we can know him personally through Jesus Christ, we can see him face to face as we look at Jesus.

'What is God like?' 'If only I could see him I would believe.' 'How can we know the truth?' These are questions that are asked over and over again. I am asked them every day as I meet people in need, perplexity and sorrow, and my answer is always the same – I point them to Jesus, and to the cross. 'But God doesn't care about me,' they complain. I remind them of what happened on the cross, and that it was for them he suffered and died, just as though there had been no one else in the world. Jesus died for the world, but the world is full of individuals, each with their own personal life to live, you and me too – and he sees us as ourselves, precious, loved, loved enough to die for. And he did! The old negro spiritual says,

Were you there when they crucified my Lord?
Were you there when they crucified my Lord?
Oh! Sometimes it causes me to tremble, tremble, tremble.
Were you there when they crucified my Lord?

Lord,
As I see your suffering, the agony you went through for me, I do tremble, with amazement, with sadness, and with love. All I can say is, Thank you for loving me so much. Thank you for dying for me. Help me now to live for you.

164

They Did What They Could
(15.40–47)

At a distance stood the group of women. Motionless, silent, apart from the sobs which came from hearts that were broken. They watched that grisly scene, their eyes fixed on the figure of Jesus, watching him die. There was Mary Magdalene who had been healed by Jesus. Mary, the mother of James and Joseph, and Salome, with other women who had come to know and love Jesus during his ministry, who had been helped, healed, comforted and listened to by him, and they in return had given him hospitality. They would have done anything for him; now all they could do was watch him die.

Many of the women who stood there that day were mothers. They knew what it was to give birth, to be overcome with love for their children, to be willing to give everything so that their children might live. They knew the intensity of love in its deepest sense. They identified with Mary, the mother of Jesus, who had stood at the foot of the cross, and who had been taken away by John to his own home, as Jesus from the cross had asked him to do. As I think of those women standing there my heart goes out to them. They were the strong ones that day, as women so often have to be in times of great suffering and distress. Look around our world today, at those areas of conflict and oppression, famine and deprivation, desperate and hopeless situations many of them. Look into the faces of the women, the waiting women. Women still carry out their vigil of love amid brutality, death and destruction, in the face of evil. Women, strong in spirit, brave, loving and determined. At the crucifixion they could do no more and no less than watch and wait, weep and pray.

Remember how Jesus had asked his disciples to 'watch and pray' in the garden of Gethsemane. They failed. He asked them again, they slept. He longed for their support, their presence, their prayers, and yet again they failed him. The women did not fail him. They must have wanted to run from that scene, close their eyes and ears to it, but they stayed, out of love. Watching what happened, watching where the body would be taken so they could care for his body, give their offerings of love, the spices for their dead Lord. What they did seemed so inadequate, of little use, but they gave what they could, and it is recorded for us as an example of love and devotion.

Sometimes when a situation seems hopeless and beyond help we freeze, do nothing, avoid it, shut it out. We can't cope with it, so we do nothing at all. Yet I find that in even the most dire of situations there is always something we can do. It may seem so paltry, even impractical, and yet I believe no act of love is wasted. No word, no tear, no prayer is ever useless. Maybe all we can do at these times is wait and watch with those who suffer, who are grief-stricken, broken-hearted. Just being there can make all the difference. I know that from my own experience.

As the women watched from a distance someone else was keeping his distance from the crucifixion, but deeply aware of everything that was happening. His name was Joseph of Arimathea. He was a respected member of the Council but also a supporter, though secretly, of Jesus. Once he heard that Jesus was dead he did an amazing thing. In a way he 'burned his boats', for he went to Pilate and asked for the body of Jesus so he could give him a decent burial. That very act marked him out as a follower of this now dead Jesus, leaving himself wide open to the same fate, had Pilate so chosen. Why did Pilate allow him to have the body? Was it merely that he saw no harm in releasing a dead Jesus – for dead men pose no threat to anyone? Or maybe it was Pilate's way of acknowledging that at least Jesus deserved a reverent resting place. After all, he had found no fault with Jesus, but had allowed himself to be swayed by the crowd's demands. As Joseph stood before him it could have been he admired the courage of the man, and so allowed the request. We don't know the reason, all we know is that Joseph was given the permission he asked for, and courageously and lovingly took down the body of Jesus from the cross, and laid it in his own tomb, the tomb he had prepared for his own death in the future. Little did he realise as he placed the body in the tomb that that place would become not the sad memorial for a dead leader, but a joyous reminder of the resurrection. The tomb would be empty very soon, because the Lord would rise from the dead. There would be no need for a tomb and grave clothes, death itself could not hold Jesus. At the time, though, Joseph did not have an inkling of what was to come. He just did what he could, no doubt regretting his failure to acknowledge Jesus in life. Now all he could do was acknowledge him in death and honour his memory.

Joseph would have a second chance to meet Jesus and to acknowledge him as his living Lord and Saviour. One legend says that Joseph was sent to Britain in AD 63 and founded the first Christian settlement in this country. Another says he brought the Holy Grail to England. Whatever happened, we can be sure he was no longer a secret believer but a public witness to the risen Lord.

Joseph did what he could. It may have seemed 'too little too late', but his courageous witness was to prove to be one of the great acts of all time. His example has inspired many a timid soul, given courage to those who felt they had forfeited their opportunity to serve the Lord by their lack of nerve in the past. Today you and I have the chance to witness to the fact that we belong to Jesus, that he is our Lord. Never mind yesterday, or whether it seems 'too little too late'. Remember Joseph of Arimathea, with everything to lose, but he took heart, took courage – and the rest, as they say, is history!

Lord,
There have been so many times when I could have stood up for you, but failed. When faced with a difficult situation I have lost my nerve, kept silent because I was frightened to speak. Those times I could have done something, said something, but what use was it? What difference could my paltry offering have made? It seemed pointless and hopeless so I turned away, and so turned away from you.
Those women stood firm, they kept faith, and stood by you. Joseph, well he somehow found the strength to be bold before Pilate, the courage to be publicly seen as your man. Yesterday I may have failed you, but you have given me today, through their examples, a renewed desire and intention to stand up and be counted, to show the world I belong to you.
I don't want to waste it,
grant me the courage to make it,
for love of you,
who died for me.

Just a Woman's Story
(16.1–11)

The women watched everything that happened. Their eyes and their hearts were fixed on Jesus. They watched him nailed to the cross, they watched him die. They watched as his dead body was taken down from the cross, and they watched where his body was placed by Joseph of Arimathea. They watched as the tomb was sealed by that huge round stone. At last Jesus could rest in peace, in dignity and in private, in death.

Why did the women watch so intently? Why did they follow to the tomb? Because they had loved Jesus in life, and loved him in death, and they wanted to make sure they knew exactly where his final resting place was to be so that they could carry out those last loving rites of annointing his body. So on the Sunday morning the two Marys set off to where they knew the body of Jesus was – but they had a problem. Two women would be incapable of moving that boulder that lay across the tomb entrance, separating the dead from the living. In their anxiety to get to the tomb they had forgotten that vital point.

All four Gospel accounts describe that early morning visit to the tomb. Matthew tells us there was a guard of soldiers as well as the stone across the entrance, to make sure the friends of Jesus did not remove his body and say he was alive; and that there was an earthquake which frightened the soldiers. Whatever the details, one thing is certain. When the women arrived the stone was rolled away, and the body had gone. Instead, an angel spoke to them, telling them not to be afraid, for

Jesus had been raised from the dead, and they were to go and tell the disciples – including Peter. The women were petrified. They, who had watched so carefully, who knew what had happened to Jesus, their minds could not cope with this amazing experience. Mark tells us they told no one because they were afraid, Matthew says they were afraid, but filled with joy too, and ran with the message. Luke says the disciples thought what they said was nonsense, and John that Mary Magdalene ran first to Peter and John and then ran back to see for themselves. A woman's story – who would believe women? The testimony of women was not accepted in a Jewish court; it was a male society, only men could be relied on, they were strong, sensible, endowed with intelligence and understanding, but women . . .

Yet it was to a woman, Mary Magdalene, that Jesus first appeared after his resurrection from the dead. No one believed her story. After all, look at her reputation, what she had been before she had met Jesus during his ministry. She had problems then, terrible problems; but Jesus hadn't looked at the problems, he looked at her, the real Mary. He drove out 'seven demons'; whatever they were, they left her at his command and she became a new woman, not a reformed character, but a transformed one. Jesus did not turn his back on her, he met her and healed her, and gave her a new start. She found in him her saviour, her rescuer, and so became one of his faithful followers and supporters.

Jesus gave Mary the honour of being the first witness of his resurrection, and of being the first evangelist – the bearer of good news. She would have loved to have kept Jesus to herself, to have remained with him, but, as we are told in John's account of their meeting, he said, 'Do not hold on to me', giving her the command, 'Go and tell my brothers . . .' In joyful obedience she went and told them, but they were mourning for their dead Master, they could not believe her story. It was impossible. No one rises from the dead, and if they did, would they choose to come back in such a manner, giving messages to a woman?

Maybe it was not the way they or we would have chosen, but then it is not what a person has been, nor their position in life that counts with God. He sees the heart. His yardstick is that of loving obedience. Paul, writing to the Christians in Corinth, had to remind them of that fact, pointing them back to their own beginnings: 'Now remember what you were, my brothers, when God called you. From the human point of view few of you were wise or powerful or of high social standing. God purposely chose what the world considers nonsense in order to shame the wise, and he chose what the world considers weak in order to shame the powerful' (1 Corinthians 1.26–27).

God chose an ordinary young girl called Mary to be the mother of his Son Jesus, who was to see the light of day in a stable. Another Mary, thirty-three years later, was chosen to be the bearer of the good news of the risen Lord, receiving her commission outside an empty tomb. What a foolish way of handling the two most stupendous messages of all time! But then, in Paul's words again, 'What seems to be God's foolishness is wiser than human wisdom, and what seems to be God's weakness is stronger than human strength' (1 Corinthians 1.25). God calls whom he will. He calls you and me to serve him, to share the good news. The qualifications he sets are love and obedience, no less and no more. The rest is in his hands. He provides all we need to do his will.

Father,
Thank you for calling me to serve you, to share
Jesus with those I meet. Give me the spirit of
loving obedience that I may joyfully and
faithfully be the bearer of good news, however
and wherever you choose.

Dead or Alive?
(16.12–18)

When Mary Magdalene burst excitedly upon the disciples of Jesus with the news that he was alive, she was not given an enthusiastic reception. Quite the opposite – they did not believe her. It would take more than the story of an over-emotional woman to convince them that someone they had seen executed, who had been certified dead by the Roman officer in charge of the execution, and had been buried in the tomb of Joseph of Arimathea by him personally, was anything but dead. Jesus had been publicly put to death, very publicly. There was no doubt that he had died on the cross. The Romans were very efficient executioners and record keepers. Besides this, the body of Jesus had been seen and handled, there was witness upon witness to testify to that. One woman's word against proven fact – she must be mad!

But then, something else, very disturbing happened – the full story is told in Luke chapter 24. Two of the followers of Jesus had left the others in Jerusalem that day to go back home to Emmaus – after all, there was no point in hanging around Jerusalem. There was nothing to hang around for, Jesus was dead and buried, and they would be best out of the way; it could be there would be a rounding up of the friends of Jesus, to stamp out any possible trouble, any reaction to his death. So they trudged wearily and sadly back home, but on the way someone joined them, talked to them about prophecies coming true, and then as they shared a meal together they realised who he was, that stranger – it was Jesus, no doubt whatsoever! So they came speeding back with the good news. It wasn't just the tale of an over-emotional woman this time, but of two very ordinary sensible men who knew sure enough who it was who had shared that road and the meal. They recounted everything that had happened on the road, described the conversation in detail, but it was no use, they were not believed any more than Mary was.

Why did the disciples not believe either Mary or the two friends? Because what they were saying was impossible. 'When you are dead you are dead'; there was no element of doubt about the death of Jesus, nothing that could give the slightest grounds for believing otherwise. Of course, it would have been lovely to have believed, it would have been wonderful if it had been true, but experience proves that these things do not, cannot, happen. 'While there is life there is hope', but when life is extinguished, of whoever it is, that is that.

People have the same problem today. They cannot believe that someone who died can be alive now. Certainly not after two thousand years! Jesus, of course, was a very exceptional person, the best man who ever walked this earth. He did the most amazing things while he was alive, he worked miracles, if you believe what it says in the Gospels, and he is still remembered today. Well, look at the organisation that was set up by his followers, it's gone on and on and on – the Christian Church, with branches everywhere.

The teaching of Jesus was unique, hard-hitting, demanding. He set standards to aim at, and if we lived by them then this world would be a very different place. Example, teaching and standards are one thing, though, but as to him being alive, well . . . Which is exactly what the disciples thought until Jesus walked in on them just as they were sitting down to a meal. He was quite cross with them, gave them a good telling off, said they were stubborn, lacking in faith not to have believed those who had already seen him. No doubt now, though, they had seen him for themselves. No need to rely on the word of anyone else, seeing was believing!

That was not the end of the matter. Jesus did not appear to them merely to make them feel better, to comfort them, or give them hope for the future; there was work to be done. They were to take out the message that he was alive and share it with the world. Now they had the task of convincing others, now they would know for themselves what it was like to have good news and, in many cases, not to be believed; but they would also have the joy of seeing the message accepted, and acted upon, they would see others come into a personal experience of Jesus. Like the Olympic flame, the news would be passed on and on. Others would take it up and out, beyond the bounds of place and race and customs and time itself.

What do you think, though?

Nicholas Brett, the editor of the *Radio Times*, wrote in March 1990, 'Whatever your beliefs, the Easter story embraces both unbelievable suffering and incredible joy.' Just before she died, the young actress Ellen Wilkie said, 'Death is a comma, not a full stop.' Bishop Colin Buchanan put it like this: 'The Jesus Christ to whom Christians respond is not the dead (though appealing) person of the past, but the living Lord of the present.' And the Archbishop of Canterbury, Dr George Carey, stating plainly and starkly his own faith said, 'I believe that Jesus was crucified, buried and that his cold, dead body was raised alive by God.' I could go on and on quoting what people have said and are saying today.

We have almost, but not quite, come to the end of our journey together through Mark's gospel, his account of 'the good news about Jesus, the Son of God'. We come to the crunch questions we must ask ourselves: 'Is it true?' 'Do I believe it?' and 'So what now?'

Dear God,
I believe . . . what do I believe, really?
I believe in God. Yes, most people say that. They like to keep on the right side of you; that is if you are you, but I am sure – well, pretty sure.
I believe in Jesus Christ, your only Son.
Of course I believe in Jesus. He was the most wonderful person who ever walked this earth, he gave us the perfect example of how to live, and I do try to follow his way. I do my best to be a Christian – although it is not always very easy, not with life as it is, and all the things that are happening, is it?
I believe he suffered, and died on the cross . . .
Yes, I believe that. What a rotten thing to do to him, and him being him and doing so much good; but then, human nature doesn't change does it? As I say, all these things happening in the world, it makes me wonder . . .
I believe he rose from the dead and is alive today.
Well, that's what the Christian faith is all about isn't it? That is what we say in the creed, that's what is really at the heart of it all. I believe it is true, I am sure it is true, but sometimes it is hard to go on believing. I want to, but . . .
Lord, help me to believe, help me to understand, help me to see . . . Jesus, now.

So What Next?
(16.19–20)

There are many times when I come to the end of a good book, an exciting film or an absorbing documentary programme on television when I say to myself, 'I wonder what happened next?' I have wanted to know more, to follow it through, to see what happened to the characters. I suppose that is why long-running series are so popular; they make you want to continue with them. I can remember as a youngster the excitement of listening each evening to *Dick Barton, Special Agent*, a radio series which always left a cliff-hanger at the end of each episode – 'Will he, won't he?' These days *The Archers* has the same effect on my husband. I know it is no use ringing or visiting certain people between seven-thirty and eight in the evening when *Coronation Street* is on, they are so engrossed in the goings-on 'down the street'.

Mark in his Gospel gives us just a peep into the events following the life, death and resurrection of Jesus. Almost all modern translations of the Gospel end at chapter 16, verse 8, when the women, having heard the news that Jesus had risen from the dead, ran away: 'So they went out and ran from the tomb, distressed and terrified. They said nothing to anyone, because they were afraid.' It is not likely that Mark would have ended his account at that point, so it would seem the original ending may have been lost. Or it could have been Mark may have been unable to finish it – perhaps he was arrested, or even put to death, for as a Christian at that time he was in constant danger, as Christians have been throughout many parts of the world ever since.

Mark 16.9–20 is regarded as an old ending, added after the original ending at verse 8, and probably derived from the other Gospel endings. Then we also have another 'old ending', two verses right at the end of the Gospel, which are a sort of précis of the women going to Peter with the news they had been given, and then of Jesus sending out the disciples with the good news. Scholars down the ages have wrestled with various possible explanations, and I can offer no new light on anything they have discovered, but what if Mark had only intended to write of the events which finished with the women running from the tomb, does it really matter?

Lord Blanch, who has made Mark's Gospel a lifetime study, has this to say in *Encounters with Jesus*:

It was enough for him (Mark) that the disciples would see Christ again. Failures, misunderstanding, the flight, the denial and even the betrayal, would be washed away in the transforming presence of the one whom, for all their inadequacies, they loved and adored. They would be back in Galilee, the past undone, back on the scene of so many wonderful works, of gracious teaching and rich companionship. He had been dead (of that there was no doubt) 'and behold I am alive for ever and ever' (Revelation 1.18). But Mark looked beyond even that ravishing prospect, to the consummation of history, when he would come on the clouds, and every eye would see him, even those who pierced him, and all the peoples of the earth would mourn because of him (Revelation 1.7). Then would be fulfilled the prophecy of Jesus on the Mount of Olives. He had foretold that 'men will see the Son of Man coming in clouds, with geat power and glory.

And he will send his angel and gather his elect from the four winds, from the ends of the earth to the ends of the heavens' (Mark 13.26–27). That would be the last great encounter when the heavens roll back and the earth is stilled, and Jesus is seated at the right hand of God.

For us today, we can read the other Gospel accounts, Matthew, Luke and John. We can discover 'what happened next' through the Acts of the Apostles, as the followers of Jesus, in the power of the Holy Spirit, set out and continued with the work entrusted to them. We have the various letters to early Christians (the epistles) which help us to understand their problems, the situations and ideas they had to contend with, the battles they had to fight, the victories they won and the price they paid. Then we have the Revelation to John, while he was imprisoned on the island of Patmos, at a time when Christians were being so badly persecuted for their faith. He 'saw an open door in heaven'. It was as though the curtain between earth and heaven was pulled back, just for an instant, and John was able to glimpse the indescribable glory of God, and by God's grace record for us something of that vision, that glory. A vision beyond words – that is why perhaps we find it hard in places to understand its total significance.

A glimpse of the future – but you and I live today, towards the end of the twentieth century, and I write in a decade which has been designated a 'decade of evangelism' or a 'decade of evangelisation'. So what is our gospel? Have we got any good news for those around us, who live next door, up the road, in our community? What have we to say to the neighbour who is overcome with grief at receiving bad news of a loved one's accident, death or disaster?

179

What can we say about the events in our country today, to people who struggle for economic survival, who are homeless, jobless, futureless? What have we to say to those who are looking for solutions to the continual crisis upon crisis, those who are given responsibility for other people's lives? What can we say to those who are without the basics of life, to the starving, the oppressed, the rootless, and the forgotten people? Where is the good news? Is there any ray of hope or understanding in a world which seems to have lost its way?

Yet the good news of Jesus Christ has not changed. Mark tells it just as it is. He hardly pauses to stop for breath, so eager is he that we should have the opportunity to meet Jesus for ourselves, know exactly what being a follower entails, and glimpse the glorious possibilities that lie before us if we are willing to 'travel light' in his company. It does not matter whether we are rich or poor, it is still for us. If Jesus had a 'bias to the poor', maybe it was because there are far more poor people than rich people; but it depends how you define 'poor' and 'rich'. It is all relative. Leslie Stanbridge, Archdeacon Emeritus of York, wrote in a recent article:

It was no accident that we first heard of Yuppies in England's eighties. No mistake, for the many who had money, life in Thatcher's England was good, and there were unbelievable luxuries which we came to take for granted. That is, of course, only part of the tale. Through the eighties we also had an England where newly-weds could not face the high mortgages, and village children were priced out of their homes which they had wanted to buy. But most of us were well fed and well heeled. So were many in the time of Jesus. If he spent a great deal of time

180

on those at the bottom of the pile he didn't ignore what he saw as the plight of those at the top. . . . There's no doubt about Jesus' call to travel light, not only to money and possessions, but reputation, dignity, social standing and the busy practice of religion too, these can be luggage that dominates a person's life, occupies all his time and energy and simply stops him from the business of living – living for God.

We all carry far too much luggage around. It drags on us, holds us back, gives us backache and heartache, ulcers and sleepless nights – but will we put our luggage down? Life is not meant to be played out as in an airport departure lounge, or train terminal, but in God's world, free to be ourselves, free to serve, free to live. Sadly, we so often prefer to stand still, holding on to our luggage rather than enjoy the life we have been given, failing to realise the truth of the old saying, 'This life is not a dress rehearsal, it's for real!'

It is for real! So is the call of Jesus to you and to me, now. 'Come with me,' he says. He promises he will be with us every step of the way, and will never leave us. He does not guarantee us an easy path – and Mark in his Gospel account has not hidden anything from us of the high cost of following Jesus, but neither has he hidden from us the great joy and wonder of discipleship, the enormous privilege of travelling light with Jesus in the company of others who have responded to his call also. We are entrusted with carrying, sharing and living 'the sacred and ever-living message of eternal salvation'.

Here is the good news, here is real and lasting hope, for all people for all time. Mark passes it on to us through his Gospel, hands it on; now it is up to us. There is no time to lose; it is a matter of life or death. We can walk away sad, like that rich young man Mark told us about, or walk with Jesus, who has died, is risen and will come again.

I made my decision over forty years ago, and have never regretted it. Each day is an adventure, because it is lived in the company of Jesus my Saviour and my Lord, who says, 'Come with me.' Who knows where he will take me yet? I am content to leave that to him! And I know, too, that the best is still yet to be – a glorious hope indeed! I pray it may be yours as well.

Almighty God,
You have enlightened your holy Church through the inspired witness of your evangelist, St Mark. Grant that we, being firmly grounded in the truth of the gospel, may be faithful to its teaching both in word and deed, through Jesus Christ our Lord.

*(Collect for St Mark the Evangelist's Day
from the Alternative Service Book)*

Lord,
Thank you for inviting me to come with you,
to travel light,
to share your life,
to show your love,
to proclaim your good news
in word and deed.
Give me the strength
to say yes and mean it,
to mean it and to do it,
to do it for your praise and your glory,
this day and always.
Amen

Also published by

TRI∧NGLE

LOSING AND LIVING
Thoughts on every kind of grieving
by David Maldwyn Owen

A collection of prayers, readings and poetry about all kinds of grieving, from bereavement to losing your job.

GROWN MEN DO CRY
Stories of a vicar's life
by Roy Catchpole

Tales of parish life from the Church of England's only ex-convict vicar.

BEGINNING WHERE I AM
Meditations for young people
by Godfrey Holmes

Meditations and prayers for a wide range of modern situations, with suggestions for beginning your own prayer life.

NOT ALWAYS MURDER AT THE VICARAGE
A view of clergy marriage today
by Steve Ann Henshall

An up-to-date look at what it is really like to be a clergy wife or husband.

Also: Margaret Cundiff's five other books
(see page ii)

TRI∆NGLE
Books
can be obtained from
all good bookshops.
In case of difficulty,
or for a complete list of our books,
contact: SPCK Mail Order
36 Steep Hill
Lincoln LN2 1LU
(tel: 0522 527 486)